C000263818

PERSO
MAST

AND THE TRAINING OF THE

MAGUS
WITHIN

JOHN SHANGO

First published in 1998 by
PURE POWER PUBLISHING
1st Floor, 14-15 Church Green East,
Redditch, Worcs. B98 8BP

© John Shango 1998

All rights reserved. No part of this book may be reproduced or
transmitted in any form or by any means, electronic or mechanical,
including photocopying, recording, or by any information retrieval
system without the written permission of Pure Power Publishing,
except where permitted by law.

ISBN 0 9532655 0 1
British Library Cataloguing-in-Publication Data
A catalogue record for this book is available from
the British Library

Printed and bound by Redwood Books
+44 (0)1225 769979

Cover design and typesetting by Pathway Designs
+44 (0)181 893 2744

CONTENTS

Personal Mastery and the Training of the Magus Within

INTRODUCTION

Personal Mastery is a handy description for the state we have attained when we are able to reach out and go beyond the limitations of our mechanical nature - the automatic responses imposed on us by social, genetic, physical, environmental and astrological conditioning. It represents a flowering of our essence as human beings, the claiming of our spiritual inheritance as transcendent entities capable of overcoming all and any of the limitations that otherwise tie us to the material plane of consciousness and existence and the physical laws which operate within that universe.

In industrialised society the quality and extent of our education, our culture, our social and our family life are dictated primarily by economic and practical, rather than spiritual and creative demands. We have been taught to believe that magic and the magical are mere superstition and that the miraculous is the sole preserve of science. Healthy scepticism has, as a consequence, become degraded to an attitude where only 'scientific' explanations are acceptable. This book is therefore written not merely for those steeped in 'New Age' thought but also and perhaps especially for those who are committed to a down to earth and practical vision of the world. For there is nothing wrong with that viewpoint. Any one viewpoint only limits us when we ignore the fact that any one way of seeing is also a way of not seeing. If we choose to have regard only for concrete and empirically verifiable facts then our world comes to consist entirely of information satisfying such concrete criteria. I have been there. If I could not kick an object it did not exist. Let us recognise that it is merely a matter of our personal choice which viewpoint or viewpoints we subscribe to, and when.

It has been said by more than one guru and channelled entity that we come to teach in the world that which we have most need to learn ourselves. That I needed to learn so much myself I hope suggests that what I have to teach may be of benefit to many. And yet the message I bring to you in this book and in my workshops is actually very simple. So I thank my readers and workshop participants for their kind expressions of appreciation for my work. They remind me that it is never merely the content of the message that changes us. It is the emotional charge with which the message is communicated and within which it takes its meaning that has the power to impact upon us.

There are of course many diversions which can so easily engage our attention and deny us our personal mastery in any one lifetime. Once we become hooked on drugs, food, sex, adulation, money, power, football, spirituality or any other addictive experience it requires enormous effort to escape. Much of our progress involves identifying such snares and recognising that they lie waiting to entrap the unwary. The downside, of course, is that most people are to a degree addicted to one or more of these snares and if you exhibit any signs of radical detachment from addictions you tend to be thought of as something of an oddity. Tough.

But we do have a powerful tool to employ in our struggle against the hooks and snares that lie in wait for us - our will; our ability to choose freely. There is no power on Earth or elsewhere that is greater than this. If we feel trapped and unable to change our lives then we tend to regard ourselves as helpless, the subject of other wills. But the reality is that it is our own previous choices, our own previous expressions of our will that now imprison us.

Through a hundred, a thousand previous choices, we have created the circumstances in which we now find ourselves and if we are now imprisoned then we are trapped only by the determination and the persistence with which we ourselves have built the bars which now surround us. Our fight is therefore not against others but rather against ourselves - against that part of us that has accepted the limitations which through a change in our belief we come to recognise as optional rather than obligatory. Thus we see it is not our will or lack of it that is at fault, it is rather our lack of clarity which causes us to choose unwisely and thereby create the circumstances that are now not to our liking. Thus empowerment and increased clarity must and do walk hand in hand together.

Our progress to mastery requires us to learn how to handle the stickiness of the material plane. It provides us with the opportunity not merely to talk about our mastery, but to demonstrate it conclusively in a challenging environment. Power is developed through overcoming restriction. We must demonstrate our power; we must walk our talk. I wish you well on your journey.

Personal Mastery and the Training of the Magus Within

CHAPTER
1

WHERE DO WE START?

There are many starting points. Each person chooses his or her own. It may be the death of someone close; it may be financial disaster, redundancy or the breakdown of a relationship. It may merely be the reaching of a certain age - the proverbial mid-life crisis - that prompts us to re-evaluate our life's direction and purpose. Such events of themselves are not enough to begin the process. In addition, a decision has to be made. It may be the first really honest, conscious decision that we have ever made; the long awaited affirmation that we do have the power to determine the course of our lives and that we shall do something about it.

Once that decision has been made there may be false starts or illusory advances. There may be apparent reversals - movement which appears to take us to a point further back than where we had assumed we had begun. We may be so unsure of the 'correct' direction to take that we embark on numerous wild goose chases. But none of this matters. Our bumpy start merely serves to illustrate that we have further to travel than we had anticipated; that our perceptions require more correction than we had assumed. And such reversals will nearly always occur, for the time span, the complexity and the enormity of the cosmos is infinitely greater and more demanding than the naive understanding that we have at the start of our journey. It is precisely because our journey is one away from illusion and limitation and towards clarity and freedom that we are unable to judge at the outset the length and complexity of the path we have to follow. Indeed, it is a sign of definite progress when we come to realise just how far we do have to travel and when the road begins to appear even longer than before.

And yet no matter how far the road extends in front of us there is no road so long as the one that has never been trod, no journey so difficult as the one that forever remains imaginary. We have at least and at last and for the first time perhaps embarked on a journey that lifts us away from the backwaters and eddies of life that have held us stuck close to the river bank and have instead plunged into the fast flowing mainstream.

I sometimes describe the journey into spiritual awareness and personal mastery as analogous to the journey through a tree to its roots; through the capillaries of a vast and incredibly complex tree with innumerable branches. Some of us are placed at the outer edge of the tree on small branches. In this position we are so far from the trunk there is little movement in the sap indicating the route we must take. And because there are so very many small branches and twigs each choice we make can take us even further from the trunk; even further away from our destination, or if we are fortunate, a little onward toward the main trunk of the tree and our destination.

This journey also serves to illustrate that at some point in our personal evolution the clarity or obscurity of our vision was irrelevant. It could not prevent us from taking 'wrong' turnings. The sheer number of 'wrong' turnings available could not but lead us astray. At the outset it is little more than chance which determines the direction we shall take; which pathway we decide to choose. Our journey involves a passage through the realms of materiality which at first leads us astray before we later learn to transcend its own peculiar demands and difficulties. So, in the outer branches of the tree we create pain for ourselves and others as we twist and turn, trying to handle with our lack of wisdom and faulty perception the innumerable decisions imposed on us by everyday life and frequently failing. But slowly the feedback of our choices, informs us that our route is mistaken, the choices we have made, flawed. Slowly our spiritual essence acquires the ability to work within and ultimately transcend the limitations of the material plane. We learn the route at first through trial and error and later on by the clarity of our informed perception and the conscious focus of our will.

Those who some describe as evil are those who have taken more than an average number of wrong turnings in their journey. Instead of a steady approach to the source, their choices have taken them further and further away from it, so far away that their spiritual essence has all but forgotten its mission. Instead of a journey towards unity there arises a search for separation and goals which are more purely materialistic. Eventually at such points on the very outermost branches there arises the only true realisation there can be: that a dead end has been reached and the only route available is backward. Those that some would describe as good are merely those who by luck and by judgment have found their way into the larger, stronger branches of the tree where the flow is greater; the direction clearer and where the route onward down the main trunk is clear. Having made few false moves they are relatively unscarred by their experiences. They have caused little hurt to themselves or others.

No route is actually more preferable than any other. The tortuous, painful and 'evil' route teaches lessons that can never be lost or forgotten; creates teachers who understand the frailties of others; who can understand and forgive the aggression, the greed, the failure, the fear, the pain inflicted because they themselves have created and suffered that pain. The easy, straightforward route creates teachers with a rare clarity of perception; refreshing in the pureness of their vision, but perhaps naive and lacking in understanding.

Our progress towards personal mastery involves a persistent yearning to become all that we are capable of becoming - a yearning to be reunited with the God within us. That yearning, pursued with commitment and vigour creates the conditions out of which positive results flow naturally. The path onward may be difficult, beset with upsets and obstacles, uneven growth and growing pains, but so long as the intention remains firm, the changes in the practical circumstances of our life must follow as certainly as night must follow day.

The road you have travelled to this point is easy for you to trace, but right now you may be sadly misinformed by your ego as to the stage you have reached in your quest for personal growth. If you wish to measure this you must consider not the skills or possessions or power that you have acquired but rather the degree to which you have been able to leave behind past constraints and limiting beliefs. You may learn how to hypnotise, how to heal, how to use the tarot. You may become an NLP Practitioner or a personal development guru, but no matter how many skills you acquire they may merely serve to enhance the size and reinforce the strength of the slag heap that lies in wait for you to remove.

Personal mastery involves first the undoing of the perceptual framework that you have created. You cannot sew a new patch onto old clothing. The new cloth tears away from the old. The pursuit of mastery requires you to strip away the old cloth; it requires you to undertake the conscious, steady and systematic elimination of those aspects of your personality which you have come to recognise as mechanical, negative, separating and limiting. As these facets of our personality begin to lose their importance we begin to uncover our essence - the naked unadorned and undeniable you; the you that is everlasting, limitless, and functions within the realm of the complete freedom that you are on the way to discover. And it is precisely because that advance primarily consists in the stripping away of those things which need to be left behind, rather than in grasping those which we consider we should acquire, that our starting point is so very often signaled by financial or emotional loss, or both. It is in coming to terms with that loss that we learn to function without the illusion of security offered by financial, emotional and psychological crutches.

It is in the process of losing the illusory that we are forced to rely on our inner essence, on that part of ourselves that may have lain near dormant for years. We then become aware that we are far stronger than we had imagined, so much freer than we had understood. All we come to lose is that part of ourselves that believed it needed support. Instead, we regain the knowledge that who we are is not contingent upon our financial or emotional status, not dependent upon whether we have a loving wife and 2.4 children, not reliant upon our success in amassing wealth, a comfortable house and a smart car. Our happiness - unless we choose to limit ourselves accordingly - is not determined by such circumstances but flows outward from us as an expression of who we are. In losing the illusory what we gain is an appreciation of who we really are - not creatures of blood, flesh, bone, emotions and thoughts circumscribed and limited by physical constraints and laws. We come to understand that our identity is preserved irrespective of the status granted us by our peers, our employers or the economy; that we really are fundamentally spiritual entities carrying within us the infinite divine spark.

Personal Mastery and the Training of the Magus Within

CHAPTER
2

POWER BUILDING PRINCIPLES

FREEDOM OF THE WILL

Pre-determination - the notion that all events are caused (pre-determined) by antecedent events - is an attractive philosophy within a technological society since it seems to no more than repeat the basic scientific assumption that cause and effect are inextricably linked. With an unbroken chain of cause and effect and a perfect knowledge of all the relevant causes it becomes at least theoretically possible to predict future events with absolute certainty. This mechanistic type theory therefore makes choice merely an illusion. What appears to be choice is no more than a feeling that arises in certain known conditions - no more than the event which immediately precedes a 'Y' junction in our destiny. The road we choose to follow from that junction is thus inevitable, pre-determined by all kinds of factors some of which contemporary science could point to.

But if all that we do is ultimately pre-determined by our genes, by our upbringing, by sociological, physical and other factors then the concept of freedom of will disappears. Choices, decisions cease to be real categories of events but mere steps in one long causal chain of inevitable events. How then can we realistically have freedom of our will if all our choices are predetermined? And if there is no true freedom of the will, then we can never hold people to be accountable for their actions; we can no longer call people morally or in any other way responsible for what they do, for they always have the perfect excuse 'I had no choice'. Of course, this does not prevent us from locking people up whose behaviour is inconsistent with the existence of a civilised society. It just means that we can no longer talk in terms of 'punishment' or give vent to our moral outrage. Perhaps this viewpoint is not such a bad thing ?

THE POWER TO CHOOSE

But the problem with the pre-determinist position is not that it is illogical but rather that it is based on a purely mechanistic view of what it is to be human. It is a dry and unexciting commentary which suggests that only a morality based solely on day to day pragmatism is of value. It is a viewpoint which pays no homage to the possibility of our transcendent nature and which instead creates and sustains the vision of man as a creature subject always to physical limitations and laws. The birth of personal power therefore begins with an affirmation that choice is possible, and continues with the conscious acceptance of that responsibility. The affirmation of our power to choose is therefore itself an affirmation of our transcendent nature. The First Law of Power therefore reads Affirm your power to choose. Say to yourself 'I have a choice here', 'I am free to choose', 'I am willing to choose'.

It is therefore necessary to step aside from the backwater of belief represented by the predeterminists position - no matter how much intellectual, scientific or philosophical credence we give it. At a personal level we must reject absolutely any attitude, viewpoint belief expression or assumption which implies that we are not free to choose. Statements given by those who our powerless are frequently, you will begin to notice, couched in terms like 'I had to do.....' or 'I didn't have any choice', 'I must do.....', 'the cup slipped'. These are all affirmations of powerlessness given as excuses for past or intended behaviour.

The corollary of the First Law of Power therefore reads 'To deny your power to choose is to become ineffective'.

To begin bringing power into our lives we therefore need do no more than assert our power to choose, to affirm our freedom to exercise our will. Whether or not you now or at sometime in the future will come to believe that this freedom is something infinitely more powerful than a mere idea is in a way not even important. What is important is that you should act and manage your life right now AS IF it were true. By accepting the belief that you are truly free to choose (even if only as a test or as an operational premise) you will begin to access the power that flows from this powerful affirmation.

You deny your power to choose when you attribute your circumstances to the will of another, the working out of destiny or the random play of events. Many people believe and feel that they have little control over their lives, little power to choose - that the forces at work influencing what happens to them and their families are simply to big, too cumbersome, too important for them to have any significant impact. And in that belief they create, affirm and sustain their own powerlessness.

In fact, there is no force in the cosmos greater than the power of will, of choice. It overrides and is capable of freeing you from limitations of birth, sociological, astrological, psychological and all other factors. It is the key to access power - the very source of creation. When expressed in the unbending power of intent it can perform miracles. The will that is free is truly free - the will that is enslaved is prisoner indeed. Your will can exist at all times and in all circumstances; it is not contingent upon outward physical constraints; merely upon its own integrity. If therefore you choose to deny it then the cosmos will hand out to you exactly what you have chosen - powerlessness.

Unless you accept all antecedent events and circumstances in your life as the product of your own power - your own choices - and accept responsibility for them, then you deny the power that brought those events and circumstances into fruition. Your ability to nurture and exercise power will remain limited for you have given your power away to other people, other events, other forces that you say have created your circumstances for you. You deny your power when you blame another for your present sorry state, for you offer up that blame as an explanation, as an excuse for your predicament. Instead, embrace your pain, your imbalance, your disadvantages, your wounds as your own. Never deny your power to create your circumstances. That you have created a mess for yourself is not a denial of your power but rather an example of how unclear perception and a shaky unfocussed will creates a screw up.

Our will is a power to employ; a resource to be recognised, developed, disciplined and turned into a mighty force. Our will is the force which directs our actions, which enables us to go beyond everyday reality; to ignore statistical improbabilities and to seize the slimmest of opportunities - the one square centimetre of chance that presents itself at a crucial time and carries within it the possibility of freedom from all constraints.

ACCEPT RESPONSIBILITY

By accepting responsibility you affirm that you have the power needed to perform the tasks dictated by the role you play. By accepting responsibility for your life as it is right now you affirm and acknowledge the power that right now lies dormant and unused within you. Yes, you may be disadvantaged, yes, you may be impoverished, yes there may be an economic recession, yes you may be the product of a broken home, yes you may have been abused as a child but no, on the path to your personal power none of it may be used as an excuse for your plight - these circumstances are the challenges that you as a warrior must confront and embrace in this lifetime. By accepting responsibility for your life - warts and all - you allow in your ability to change it. Until then your power to do so belongs to others.

The man or woman in pursuit of personal mastery - the spiritual warrior - does not bemoan his lack of intelligence, the poverty of his parents, the love that was denied him as a child, his lack of opportunities or money. He accepts the advantages and the disadvantages with which he awakens with equanimity. He accepts who and where he is right now. His task - the task of all of us - is to transform ourselves. The Second Law of Power therefore reads Accept responsibility for everything you do, for everything you are, for everything you say. Its corollary states To deny responsibility is to deny your power

Accepting responsibility signifies that we accept the rules of the game of life. Acceptance enables us to go onto the field and join in. For so long as we avoid taking responsibility so long do we remain sidelined, a substitute that never gets called into play. A player can, after all, only ever be a person who has agreed to accept the rules of the game.

Do not despair that in accepting responsibility the full weight of your present apparent failure will bear down heavily upon you and that you will crumple under its weight. Remember instead that what you have created is a powerful demonstration of the incorrect and unconscious deployment of your power. With the increasing clarity of your perception and your consciously focused intent your power is easily capable of creating an entirely new set of circumstances.

Acceptance is generally regarded as a passive process, so go beyond mere acceptance of the responsibility that may be thrust upon you. Reach out and seize the responsibility for your plight in anticipation of the power that will then come to you.

I have witnessed head colds and hay fever disappear, blotchy and spotty facial complexions clear up, assertiveness and energy spring into being all within a few days of responsibility being seized. Even unaccustomed responsibility taken on at work can have dramatic effect. The voluntary acceptance of responsibility puts us on the line; in a position where we and perhaps others stand or fall by the decisions we make. And it is in precisely those circumstances that we begin to reach out and go beyond our usual fearful state and access the energy and power we need to successfully accomplish the task.

Accepting responsibility says to the cosmos "Leave it to me, I have the power, the resources, the commitment and the will to fix it; I will do whatever is necessary to achieve the required result". Responsibility therefore also assumes commitment and turns away needless help. The extraordinary thing is that, whether or not you actually have the power, the energy or the resources at the outset, the very fact that you have taken on the responsibility enables you to access all those qualities very quickly. Accepting responsibility is therefore an incredibly powerful affirmation. By affirming we have all we need, that is exactly what we get.

Now consider what happens when, perhaps because of our well meaning sentimentality (but actually our lack of clarity) we prevent others from accepting or acquiring a degree of personal responsibility, when we persist in giving help when not help but self reliance is needed. By offering or giving such unnecessary help we assert "We cannot leave this to you; you are incapable, you are powerless, you are ineffective". And sure enough, when we treat people like that, that is how they become. To provide sufficient resources to 'prime the pump' is to truly help. But to provide resources which are within a person's own ability to acquire is to disempower. It is very often a fine line that has to be drawn between helping and choosing not to. This illustrates the principle that a good quality turns to a bad quality when employed to excess or, in the words I think of Alfred Lord Tennyson "God fulfils himself in many ways lest one good custom should corrupt the world".

THE STATE AND RESPONSIBILITY

For many years now there have been forces at work in most of the western democracies which serve to disempower their citizens. What began in the UK as a modest and necessary safety net for the unfortunate has burgeoned to the point where the need for self-reliance and personal responsibility has all but disappeared, and instead the state has seemingly acquired a moral duty to provide jobs, welfare, education, benefits, medical care and a host of other services.

This increasingly paternalistic quality of the state is also seen in the extent to which it legislates to protect the consumer against almost every imaginable pitfall or absence of good judgment, against every tiger and bear lying in wait outside the citizen's cave. Each piece of legislation is, when individually considered, no doubt of value in curing a potential wrong that one man does to another. But the overall result of such legislation is to prevent the consumer citizen from ever being responsible for his or her personal, financial or commercial decisions. There is always a person to blame other than oneself if something goes wrong.

And as the state in this way takes over individual responsibilities so it unwittingly creates more and more demands on its own resources. Its actions cease to be a temporary pragmatic response to a social problem and become instead the fulfilment of a moral obligation. The safety net for the weaker members of society to draw on becomes a "right" for all in society to claim. And so each generation becomes less self reliant and more reliant on the welfare state rather than itself. And society begins to believe its own fictions. We are told, for example, that poverty in the UK is increasing; that the rich are getting richer and the poor are getting poorer. But this is not actually happening. Polarisation of wealth into two socio-economic classes a la Marx is as dead as a doornail. What is happening is that definitions of poverty are being upgraded to keep pace with the rising standard of living. What was once a luxury - a colour television set - is now rarely absent from a household in poverty. Recent work by the Institute of Fiscal Studies evidenced conclusively that all strata in the UK are in fact becoming richer.

As the demographic profile of the developed nations changes so that fewer working people are available to support an increasing number of elderly people it becomes increasingly harder for the state to manage and share out the scarce resources entrusted to it. And as this trend continues the state has no choice but to hand back responsibility to its citizens if it is to escape bankruptcy. The beginning of this new trend was signaled by the establishment of the Child Support Agency in the UK which for the first time created a specialist agency devoted to tracing absent parents and making them pay towards their childrens' upkeep. At the time of writing discussions about limiting housing benefit are also in progress. The light is dawning as the state begins to recognise that it has no choice but to adopt policies which strengthen rather than weaken its citizens, albeit for the state's purely selfish economic motives.

In my own view a welfare policy is needed which pays attention to both the physical and the spiritual needs of those in unfortunate circumstances. There are many that object to the principle of means-testing, but what is a tax return if not a means test? If we rigorously apply means testing then the scarce resources of the state will not be wasted. What is required is a system where the receipt of welfare benefit is not a begrudging gift but a wage - albeit a low wage - given in exchange for a definite commitment of time and energy - perhaps on some social or community project such as visiting the elderly. A proper exchange of value occurs and therefore there is no disempowering effect on the recipient.

This brings us to the Third Law of Power which states that 'Fair exchange empowers'. Its corollary reads 'Excessive demands and overprotection both weaken'.

CONFRONT YOUR FEARS

Fear appears in many guises. Raw, physical fear is an emotion we all recognise. But fear can and usually does manifest itself in far less obvious ways; we learn to disguise it from others and from ourselves. We express our unwillingness to confront an issue merely in terms of our preference or inclination. We avoid telling the truth because we fear the embarrassment or emotional pain that we know will result. We avoid certain people, certain places, certain things which our bodies and or minds perceive as challenging.

By avoiding such confrontations or challenges we appear to sidestep the immediate experience of fear. But this detour in reality costs us dear in terms of the opportunities that pass us by and the problems that could have been nipped in the bud but which now fester and grow eventually into overt hostility or indeed open warfare. Every time we take that detour we affirm our weakness and voluntarily limit the extent of our actions. With repetition this self limitation becomes habitual and we create persistent patterns of avoidance behaviour. And later on we may even begin to applaud our own inability to confront issues and assert that the greater good is demonstrated by the absence of confrontation; by not making waves; by consideration for others. But of course these are not the true alternatives to confrontation. If we fail to confront issues squarely and completely then every word we utter, every movement of our body is a lie making effective communication impossible. And problems between people can only ever be solved by real communication.

So, by trying to avoid fear rather than confronting it directly we come to accept limitations on the potential range of our actions; we voluntarily curtail our freedom. The world is no longer our oyster but a much smaller neighbourhood whose boundaries are determined by our own inhibited patterns of behaviour and with whose inhabitants we are unable to effectively communicate. Our desire to avoid confrontation and the fear that entails, can become so deeply ingrained in our everyday life that we forget exactly why we are behaving as we do. Our patterns of avoidance behaviour become locked into our bodies and minds becoming blocks which deny our freedom, limit our choices and obstruct our personal and spiritual growth - and all so deeply embedded in our psyche that we experience them as immovable boundaries. And yet they are merely thoughts.

Our task then is to question ourselves, our habits, our limitations, our assumptions and our fears. We must question all that tends to inhibit our freedom of action and seek out its origin. Then we must face our fears with determination and with absolute commitment. With such commitment sufficient energy is available to break through the limits that we have laid down for ourselves. There is no hoping to avoid this issue. Confronting fear is a fundamental pre-requisite of personal and spiritual development. The Fourth Law of Power states 'Confront your fear squarely and completely and wherever it arises'; in so doing you build a larger universe to play in. I sometimes make the point slightly differently in my workshops by saying something like "I don't care if you can channel the archangel Gabriel, if you can't face a firewalk workshop you are a spiritual infant". Make no mistake, the firewalk is an obligatory part of everyone's spiritual curriculum.

FOCUS YOUR ATTENTION & YOUR ENERGY

Most people are ineffective because what power they have seeps from them indiscriminately in an unfocussed dissipation of energy. For power to be effective it must be focused. Water in the form of rain embodies little physical impact. Only when channelled and focused into the form of a mighty river can its enormous power be unleashed.

Powerful, creative acts require us to be focused. Focus involves directing our attention, our energy and our resources into a generally small and precisely defined impact zone. When this is done our energy becomes effective, capable of accomplishing the changes, the manifestations we desire. The effective focusing of energy and material resources represents one aspect of mastery at the physical level. The ability to exercise this creative control is a skill that we all must learn. The Fifth Law of Power states 'Focus your attention and energy for maximum impact'.

Many people are simply unable to bring the required degree of focus to their job, their sport or their home. They are easy to spot. Their attention span is limited; they are easily distracted, they waste time and effort and their attention is diverted by irrelevancies. They are the actors in other peoples scripts. They have little impact and exert little control over the direction of their lives. They are slaves to fashion changes; the mass to whom advertisements are directed; the receivers and consumers of pre-packaged information and views. Learning to focus energy and resources for some people requires considerable time, patience and practice. So be it.

There is a side effect of focusing our attention and energy on a specific impact zone. The area outside that zone necessarily receives less

power and energy than it received previously. Focusing our attention in
one direction necessarily involves us in withdrawing our attention from
another. A way of seeing is also a way of not seeing. Thus focus also
involves an element of blindness.

Those with an abundance of compassion who have yet to learn how to
manage their resources and focus their attention invariably say yes, yes,
yes to all the requests for help and demands that are made of them. They
spread their energy and resources increasingly thinly until eventually
they become unable to spread their resources any thinner. They become
incapable of helping anyone or managing even their own lives
effectively. They become unable to fulfil the numerous commitments
that they have made and consequently become unreliable and powerless
to help anyone at all. Or they strive and strive to fulfil the huge demands
being made of them until eventually they crack - they suffer a nervous
breakdown, executive burn out or simply do a disappearing act. This
brings us to an important implication of the Fifth Law:

The corollary of the Fifth Law of Power states 'To focus your attention
and energy you must say No'. For many people this is exceedingly
difficult. Nevertheless it is an essential part of being able to manage our
energy and resources that we are able to say 'No' when necessary. For
many years I was plagued by telephone calls from those who wished me
to advertise in their publications. I would find it difficult to simply say
'No'. I would find myself giving long winded and unnecessary
explanations seeking to justify my reluctance and in the process wasted
everyone's time. Now I simply say 'No, thank you' politely but with the
full power of my intent behind it. The conversation is invariably over
within 10 seconds. Of course, it is the tone of your voice which
communicates your intent and there are some who will teach you how to
model such things. That's fine for some but to me it seems like learning
a skill, acquiring another layer of programming to further complicate
our social relations. How much better if we strip away all that artificiality
and let our real essence shine through with all its natural power and
intent.

By revealing our focus we reveal ourselves. Our beacon of focused intent shines outward for all to see. Naturally there are those who are unhappy about the direction revealed by the light we shine. This is inevitable. But more importantly with our focus revealed we become a point of focus for others; a light which draw others in. Often our focus is our passion. Witness those who have developed a passion for a particular hobby or for collecting. Not only can their passion invoke the interest of others but also it is extraordinary how often such people, frequently with very modest incomes amass collections worth hundreds of thousands of pounds, simply by becoming very knowledgeable in their chosen field, by being alert to opportunities and by applying such resources as they do have in a very focused way.

Focusing is clearly easy if we have a passion for the object of our focus. More difficult, but also more beneficial in terms of your personal growth is the need to focus on tasks about which we are not inspired. The old saying 'If a job is worth doing, then it is worth doing well' sums this up. If we choose to undertake a task then we must commit ourselves, focus ourselves 100% to achieve that task in the best possible way. It does not matter whether the task is doing the washing up or designing a safe nuclear reactor, whether we like the task or hate it. Once we are committed to the task our attention must be total. Attention, attention, attention said the Zen Master.

When we apply the full power of our focused intent to the task, certain things happen. We learn to fulfil the task more efficiently; we innovate; we create; we develop the physical means, the mental and motor skills appropriate to the task. We discover that the reason behind our disinclination to do the task was either fear or laziness. Eventually we achieve mastery of the task and demonstrate supreme economy of effort - the mark of the true Master. Some tasks are easy to master, others more difficult and time consuming - taking years before proficiency is attained and years more before mastery is reached. But make no mistake, there are millions out there who have yet to achieve mastery even over their washing up.

The Sixth Law of Power states 'Release focus when you act'. To be focused is analogous to holding up a clenched fist. It represents the preparatory period where we marshal our resources, practice our moves, make plans, consider our position and make decisions. When that phase is complete we have to be able to recognise that fact; we have to be able to release that focus into a whirlwind of action, a spontaneous outp ouring of energy. Such release is symbolised by the open hand. If we seek to preserve our focus when the time for action has arrived we limit the outpouring of our energy and the purpose behind our focus is lost.

WILLINGNESS TO BE A CAUSE

Many people are willing to talk endlessly but are reluctant to act - perhaps excessively cautious or too fearful of the consequences to take any action. They remain stuck where they are. We must learn and be prepared to initiate action wherever and whenever our judgment determines that it is desirable. Taking action often involves being noticed, taking responsibility. When we take action we stand up and are counted; we are objects of admiration, envy and criticism and are accountable for the results we produce. Many people shrink from this public scrutiny

Willingness to take action is the readiness to act, in a sense, irrespective of the likely consequences; it is the preparedness to act not-withstanding the fear we may feel or the seriousness of the situation. It is the choice we make between being the hammer or the anvil, the doer or the done by. It is in our willingness to act that we stand in the fullest potentiality of our power. The greatest concentration of physical power on the planet - the hydrogen bomb - gained its political power only because enough people knew that there existed the political will to press the   button to unleash the ICBMs. Without that willingness to act there can be no power. Without that willingness to act we are merely wimps; responding, squealing, protesting at the way we are unjustly dealt with but ultimately doing as we are told and subject to the whim of anyone who has the will to intimidate us. The Seventh Law of Power simply reads 'Do not shrink from action'.

Nevertheless, our willingness to act can often cause us pain and difficulty - especially when our judgment to act is borne of faulty or unclear perception. But these are simply growing pains. Growth is frequently painful. If life were always easy and full of contentment there would be no incentive, no catalyst, no impetus in our lives to change and grow. Our willingness to act is often a good measure of our emotional strength and readiness to accept the pain that may be associated with the action we take.

COMMITMENT

The principles of power discussed above are in practice all closely related. As we learn to focus, to accept responsibility for our actions and acquire a readiness to initiate action so do we also become increasingly committed to achieving the goal or goals we have set ourselves. The force of our intent becomes a promise to ourselves, a vow, a commitment to undertake whatever is necessary to accomplish the task. The special meaning given by the warrior to this term must be clearly understood. To the average person the commitments that he or she make are given generally with little thought and are secretly conditional - i.e. subject to usually a host of undeclared provisos, ifs and buts which stand ready to serve as an excuse to change our minds if the going gets too rough - if the task gets a little more difficult than we had anticipated, if the resources needed to accomplish the task are rather greater than we had assumed.

Contrast this type of 'commitment' with the commitment that the warrior makes. His or her commitments are absolute and subject only to any previously announced and specified conditions that he or she may make. Thus the warrior's commitments can be relied upon, whereas those of the average man and woman cannot. Of course, since the warrior knows what it is to make a commitment, he or she tends to make commitments rather sparingly. And that means that he or she tends to get rather a lot of practice in saying 'No' - inevitable when we focus our energy and commitment.

Commitment is therefore the decision to go for it, whatever the cost. Commitment is the key that invokes extraordinary energy; the signal to self and the cosmos to employ any and all resources irrespective of the consequences or side effects to achieve the required result. It is the action command which overrides all other considerations; the ultimate focus of energy and resources. The warrior, aware of its power, commits himself sparingly and with wisdom.

In 49 BC Julius Caesar, then Military Governor of Gaul, signaled his intention to overthrow the Roman State by crossing the Rubicon river thereby entering territory prohibited him and his army. This act committed him to a course of action which could only end with success or a traitors death. That commitment, signaled in advance, galvanised his army's advance and created much of the energy for his success.

Similarly, in 1940, Rommel, then in command of the 7th Panzer Division disobeyed the orders of the German High Command to halt his breakneck advance through France. A succession of motorcycle couriers delivered written orders to him to halt his advance at certain defined points. But such was the speed of his advance that by the time the messages were received he had already passed those points, and he therefore chose to interpret the orders as being out of date. By so doing he became personally committed to the success of his attack. Failure would have meant Court Martial and a career in ruins.

One more well known example of personal commitment by a commander in wartime occurred at the Battle of Copenhagen. Nelson, second in command, was ordered to disengage from a numerically superior Danish fleet. Instead, he held a telescope up to his blind eye and denied seeing the signal to withdraw. He then pressed on with the attack achieving a notable victory.

In such examples the commanders concerned transcended their defined roles; they stopped being mere soldiers and became warriors - personally committed to victory whatever the cost. They could not excuse their behaviour as a mental aberration or a misunderstanding - the wimp's usual response to the realisation that there may be trouble ahead. Fortune favours the brave, it is said. More accurately, fortune favours the committed, for it is the committed that create the circumstances to access the personal energy, the physical, emotional and spiritual resources necessary to achieve success against apparently overwhelming odds. And it is also commitment that sometimes can unlock the power to break through self imposed or learned limitations, physical and emotional blocks and constraints. A personal example illustrates how this can work.:

For many years I suffered from a crippling emotional block which prevented me from revealing my feelings and hindered my ability to relate to others. I seemed a cold lifeless person, whereas in fact I desperately needed to allow my feelings to surface. The catalyst was a sweat lodge. A sweat lodge is a small structure looking rather like an igloo made of bent over branches covered by a thick layer of blankets. Inside the sweat lodge are crammed about 20 people sitting in complete darkness. Then, red hot stones are pushed in from outside, having been heated in a fire for several hours. Water is splashed on the stones to create an almost unbearable mixture of heat and humidity. Then a purification ritual lasting about two hours begins.

Within moments of entering the sweat lodge I began to panic. I came face to face with an almost overpowering and irrational fear of suffocation and claustrophobia, a fear which I now know is karmic in origin. My body and emotions shrieked at me to escape from the lodge. I was absolutely desperate to leave it, but having made the warriors commitment to stay in it whatever the cost I had no choice but to face my fears squarely and completely. Something had to give, and it did. I cried out, shouted, screamed unashamedly in a display of raw emotion - a display which revealed to the world all my inner fears that had hither to been hidden behind a mask. That display of emotion was like a flood bursting through a dam. Instantly, I became able to show normal emotions and could reveal myself and relate to others. By confronting directly my fear of suffocation through my commitment I overcame the emotional block which had stifled the expression of emotion for so many years. It was then that I came to realise that there really are break-throughs in personal development - that change does not happen slowly, gradually but sometimes in quite large steps. We just need to create the right impactful circumstances to create them.

The Eighth Law of Power reads: 'Commitment is the irrevocable personal pledge to employ all and any available resources, no matter what the cost, to achieve an objective'.

Commitment is implicit in the very process of decision - making. Unless we commit ourselves to our decisions we fail to make true decisions at all. In my workshops we demonstrate the required degree of commitment by bending steel rods used to reinforce concrete. We place one end of the 10mm diameter rod against the base of our throat just above the collar bone. By pushing the rod with total commitment against this soft area of windpipe we make the steel bend. Our ego thinks only about the steel rod piercing our throat. But the commitment we bring to bear enables us to go beyond that fear and bend the steel. If we really are committed then the steel rod bends without difficulty (or injury to the participant).

This implacability - or impeccability as some would call it - is beautifully illustrated by the story of how Odette Churchill, overcame her Gestapo jailers. For two years she was tortured and kept in solitary confinement. She would endlessly repeat that she had nothing to say. Years later she recalled that one summer day she saw through the open window of her interrogation room the trees in the Bois de Boulogne; their greenness and their freedom. It was then she realised that she had but one choice. As she was not going to say anything she was going to die. That acceptance made her stronger. After they had pulled out her toenails her torturers were about to begin on her finger nails, but the German Commandant ordered the torturers to stop. It was clear to him that nothing would break her implacable spirit. The Gestapo gave up on her and sent her to Ravensbruck concentration camp . She was one of only 13 women agents in France to survive the war.

If we can bring into our lives even a small part of the commitment that

Odette was able to summon when put to the test our lives will be radically transformed. Such commitment is a powerful tool because it both denies the demands of the ego and asserts the supremacy of the spirit. In the words of Jedi Master Yoda in 'The Empire Strikes back':

Try Not

Do, do

Or do not

There is no try

WILLINGNESS TO EXPERIENCE PAIN

A life without pain would be bliss. Or would it ? Pain is a warning to our senses that we are entering into an experience for which we are unprepared. This does not mean that we should necessarily avoid the experience; merely that it is likely to be painful. We often feel pain - physical and emotional - not because our bodies are about to suffer terminal damage, but rather as an indication that we are stretching our emotional and physical resources; that we are passing beyond our personal comfort zone into an arena which demands our utmost energy and such resources as we do have. By going into that zone of discomfort we often learn quickly. We grow in our awareness, in our strength and in our confidence and so after a while that zone changes and becomes part of an expanded zone of comfort. We are changed and prepared to meet new demands, new challenges.

When I was a schoolboy we were regularly sent on cross country runs. Or at least the other boys in my class were. I nearly always managed to manufacture some excuse to avoid the painful experience of running hard. And when I ran out of excuses I would manage to disappear behind a hedge and reintroduce myself into the tail end of the exhausted runners on their return. I was proud of my ingenuity - I could not have experienced more than 3 or 4 cross country runs in five years. But, as with all the principles set out in this book, the longer you avoid addressing issues, the more difficult does mastery of them become. It was not until I was about 27 years old that I decided to get myself fit, having been inspired by a book about the aerobic training regime practiced by the Canadian Air Force. With a certain degree of naiveté and an inflated idea of my physical prowess I planned a run of perhaps two and a half miles to the local park, around it, and back to my first floor flat in Kings Heath, Birmingham

With my emerging warriors will I decided that, come what may, I would run the full distance without stopping or walking - and this for a man who had probably not broken into a run or exercised for nearly 10 years. The run turned out to be the most gruelling and physically punishing experience of my life. Never, before or since, have I pushed myself physically so completely. Had I known in advance the difficulty or the physical suffering I would endure I would almost certainly not have made the commitment. But I did succeed in getting round the planned route without stopping or slowing to a walk. At the finish I was so exhausted that I crawled up the stairs to my flat, step by agonising step. It took about five minutes for me just to climb the stairs. My heart at least must have been in good shape. I do not recommend you to begin an exercise regime in this way. It could prove terminal.

Until I made that commitment to run the distance irrespective of the consequences I had not been able or ready to accept physical pain. I had accepted for all of my life up to that moment a purely self-imposed limitation, that physical exertion and the associated pain was to be avoided. This does not mean that it is right or desirable to be masochistic, merely that to voluntarily accept a degree of pain is an experience, a price to be paid, that can help us grow. And to grow stronger, it is quite often a price that we should be prepared to pay.

Some people find that it is emotional rather than physical pain that they have difficulty in accepting. For a long while I suffered from both. As related above, it took me until I was 27 before I could face physical pain and not until I was over 40 before I learned to accept emotional pain. Those that do not experience much loving care as children tend to be prone to this emotional Achilles heel. In their unbalanced search for emotional support they get entangled in unsuitable relationships yet find it overly difficult to break away from them when the relationship falters. They are unwilling to accept the emotional pain implicit when two people part.

Unless we learn our lessons as they are presented to us - and sometimes this means our willingness to pay a certain price in physical or emotional terms - the situations that arise to repeat the lessons that we fail to grasp become increasingly more severe, more confrontational and stark in their character until eventually the grossness of the situation seemingly imposed on us but actually created by our own emotional weakness forces us to perceive clearly. It is only then that we make correct but exceedingly painful decisions - decisions that would have involved us in far less heartache and pain had we the courage to accept the pain at an earlier, more appropriate time.

Clarity of perception is intimately related to the sort of person we are. If we lack the courage to confront an issue then we often rationalise away our weakness and express our desire to avoid an issue as a preference for some other (and easier) option. What we perceive is then naturally clouded by our inadequacy. Only when we become incapable of being intimidated by our fear, willing to confront all experiences with equanimity, can we see clearly.

THE FIREWALK

The firewalk is a tool which teaches teach us how to confront our fears squarely and completely. But it is much more than this. Treading on incandescent coals at a temperature of 1200 degrees we our reliant only upon ourselves; it is a demonstration of the trust we have in our transcendent nature. We do not rely on our faith in technology to open our parachute and get us down to earth safely. We rely solely on our own apparently feeble and untried resources. Our confrontation is total - we ignore the screaming demands of our fragile egos and make a massive leap of faith in our own ability.

The seminar which precedes the firewalk prepares participants both psychologically and physiologically. It places them in the empowered state necessary for them to be able to walk unharmed over the coals. This is accomplished by freeing up their beliefs about who they are and what they are capable of accomplishing and then freeing up their personal energy, often just untried and unused by a lack of expression through limited use. Sometimes I am asked about insurance by the media and by those attending firewalks. I know that some firewalk instructors offer this. I do not. To me, insurance is contrary to the very essence of the firewalk. When we arrange insurance we seek to share or avoid the responsibility for our actions and the decisions we make. By fully accepting that responsibility our call for empowerment is total and we therefore receive all the power we need to accomplish the task. The firewalk is all about accepting total responsibility for ourselves. Insurance can only ever diminish this.

I do not teach people to firewalk. That ability is a side effect of the power that we are all able to access. My role is rather to change peoples beliefs which then allows a change in energy to take place. Only a small change is needed to achieve the desired result. Nor do I in the seminar actually encourage anyone to firewalk. My role is to place the participants in a position where they are able to make an informed decision for themselves. The decision to walk is then left entirely to them.

Personal Mastery and the Training of the Magus Within

CHAPTER
3

SIGNPOSTS ON THE WAY

This chapter is about some of the experiences and some of the qualities that will arise as you journey toward personal mastery. Notice them as you experience them in your life. They are the roadside milestones, the signposts on the way.

ACTS OF POWER

Powerful acts are acts which spring not from the dictates of our mechanistic personality and ego, driven by our animalistic nature or conditioning, but those which arise from our essential self or spirit as it strives to express its unlimited nature within the stickiness and seeming constraints of the material plane. Powerful acts therefore always involve an element of detachment from the demands of the ego, and the warrior cultivates this detachment. Since the ultimate stronghold of the ego is the physical body the warrior ultimately learns to detach himself from his own death. As the warrior comes to view his own death with detachment he quickly acquires a clarity of perception unknown to the average person.

Carlos Castenada's Don Juan says that the detached man who knows he cannot escape his own death has only one thing to give substance to his existence - the power of his decisions. He has to be the master of the choices he makes. And the power of those decisions make him able to choose without regret.

A powerful act is an act which is a demonstration of clear commitment; an intentional act which binds the warrior to grasp more than his own apparent resources. For our power derives not merely from our   physical energy and resources but from our ability to become instruments of power - to become channels for it. And our ability to become channels for it depends in turn on the extent to which we are able to eradicate the tremblings of our egos and lock into the mighty energetic resources of the cosmos.

Spirit - the power that is conscious of itself - is an impersonal and emotionless force awaiting deployment. Our emotions are a reflection of the limitations and constraints which derive from our relationship with materiality - a buffer zone which releases the stresses arising from the interface between the infinite spirit and the physical constraints imposed on it. To the extent that we nurture and practice our spiritual nature to that extent do we become skilled at deploying and manifesting our personal power on the physical plane.

CLARITY OF PERCEPTION

We tend to assume that perception is a passive process, our eyes, ears and other sensory organs receiving sensory impressions with our brain merely recording those impressions as information. But perception does not work like this. Perception is actually a very active process; a process in which our beliefs and past experiences intermingle with the 'raw' data; in which the placement of meaning on that data is always inextricably linked with our perception of it. We therefore do not ever actually behold raw unprocessed data; it comes to us already pre-packaged by our predispositions.

So what are these predispositions ? One very well established aspect of perception is the phenomenon known as gestalt - the tendency for us to fill in gaps where data is missing. We often know by seeing only a small part of an object what that object is. It is not necessary for our brain to record 'unknown object' or for us to painstakingly examine every last minute detail of a chair before we are able to pronounce on its identity. The gestalt phenomena acts as a perceptual short-cut, saving us from indecision and from the timewasting involved in repeated minute examinations of similar objects. One predisposition is therefore this gestalt short cut. If we see something new which looks much like what we have seen before we automatically assume that the new object or event falls within the same category and record it as such. Our perceptions can therefore often be overly simplistic and repetitive in their nature. The raw data of the universe passes through a filter consisting of cultural values, personal priorities, beliefs, prejudices and fears. This filter sifts out and organises incoming data into categories which have personal relevance. And, of course, since most of us share similar values and priorities the filter enables us to share a common perceptual experience. One person sees much the same world as another does. This experience is referred to in the works of Carlos Castenada as the Tonal. or First Attention, and produces the ordinary, everyday reality with which we are all familiar. But, as I have said before, a way of seeing, even if held by many or all people, is also a way of not seeing. When we focus on one aspect of available experience we blind ourselves to other aspects. As we learn to acquire the perceptual pragmatism of the everyday First Attention we become unable to perceive the Nagual, or Second Attention; the naive perception which does not employ socially prescribed categories but which nevertheless reveals the underlying energetic structure of objects.

The quality of our past perception can only really be assessed when we look back from the standpoint of hopefully our present clarity. To be sure of relatively clear perception now we need to be confident that we are not living under the dominion of fear and the strategies of avoidance and self delusion that we have created for ourselves. If we are able to accept with relative equanimity both success and failure, joy and sorrow, then the chances are that our essence is sufficiently detached from our ego to allow reasonably clear perception at least within the First Attention.

SINGULARITY OF WILL

Personal power requires personal congruence. This involves the prioritization, amalgamation, subordination and sometimes elimination of the various contradictory aspects of our identity until they become a coherent singularity. The 'I' that wishes to go to bed early because of an early start the next day needs to confront the 'I' that wishes to stay up late to watch a film. One 'I' temporarily dominates the other, and then the other 'I' temporarily takes its place. In such cases it is simply the immediate environment that has changed, which first gives support to one 'I' and then the other. And so, like a ship with no engine we are blown first in one direction and then another. Gurdjieff held that these contradictions are prevented from manifesting within the human psyche by a number of 'buffers' whose purpose is to help us avoid unpleasant shocks and realisations, and the realisation of our own contradictory natures.

To remove these buffers, to work toward creating a singular 'I' or will, we can use the weapon of self-observation to note our personal inconsistencies and to create a degree of detachment sufficient to disrupt the link between stimulus and the resulting mechanical response. As our personal inconsistencies are brought to the surface we must strive to maintain our self-observation and so create and maintain a layer of consciousness separate from our mechanical, auto-responsive nature.

UNSELFISHNESS ?

We frequently associate moral and spiritual development with a person's ability to consider and care for his fellows. And, truly, it is one of the more noble aspects of human nature that we frequently cooperate and give help to others sometimes to our own detriment. But more needs to be said. Whilst clearly there is a relationship between spiritual advancement and unselfishness in some people at some times, there are other considerations. There are many who care deeply for their fellows and yet accomplish little or nothing for them, because they are unable to focus their energy and resources effectively. And there are many who give of themselves unstintingly but who fail to consider the more problematic consequences of their help.

Excessive help, as we discussed in Chapter 2, always disempowers the recipient. Help is best offered as a priming of the pump, a provision of the physical, mental and/or emotional resources sufficient to correct a temporary imbalance. I recall that as a child of about 9 or 10 years old I had a friend who received so much help from his father that he was unable to do anything practical at all - he would not attempt to make anything for himself. His fathers excessive doting help had eliminated all of his initiative. Help should be given in the same way as we should help and teach a child to become an adult - an exercise in which the adult parent acts as a catalyst for the child's self-empowerment.

And do we not know this instinctively ? Do we not find it so much easier to help someone who is clearly striving to support himself ? One might say that one warrior recognises another. Likewise, we find it easy to help those who are clearly in desperate straits. But between those polar types there is a mass of people in the world and especially in the Western European and Nordic states who have learned to rely on the state as of right; a mass whose initiative and self respect has been wiped out by the state's focus on their physical needs. In the UK there has arisen a support system which, rather than providing incentives for people to climb out of physical and spiritual impoverishment, instead encourages people to accept assistance as of right and gives more incentives for those who are without work to have children than to those who are in work. Thus we discriminate against those very people who are most likely to engender in their children qualities of self reliance, initiative and responsibility. Instead, we choose to encourage those who are destined to spread a culture of powerlessness and helplessness.

But what about those many hard working people who neglect their own yearnings, who ignore their own dreams and who strive to help others in need ? It seems to me that it makes no sense if each generation or group of people offers itself as a martyr merely to serve the next. It makes no sense if our prime moral purpose is simply to help our fellow man, for then we neglect our own development in which no other man can play such a vital role, and each man would then become a martyr to the next with the result that none is fulfiled. Each person has one task above all others which they cannot delegate - to transform themselves - to reach their highest potential, to become all that they are capable of becoming, to stretch their spiritual wings and fly. And whilst in pursuit of that transformation we come learn that the interests of one are aligned with all others; that the transformation of one assists in the transformation of all. And, of course, in the pursuit and expression of that transformation love flows outward to those in need, not merely as a mechanistic response to a moral imperative but as the natural outcome of self healing brought about by increased trust and an associated reduction in the ego's demands.

And as we increasingly leave behind our fears and mechanical responses so do we become more clear about the manner the type and the extent of help that is appropriate to give in each case. We become better able to achieve the elusive point of balance between helping and not helping, between neglecting our own needs and paying due attention to them. Balance born of clear perception and an open but wise heart is the key.

FORGIVENESS

Whenever one person suffers a wrong at the hands of another the one who suffers frequently needs to correct their own perception of events. The wrongdoer may quickly forget his wrongdoing, but unless the sufferer can leave behind the wrong it remains to smoulder and becomes a knot, a focus for negativity. Forgiveness is the process by means of which we let go of that knot; the act of transcending the frame of reference created by the past incident(s) which hold us in their power.

Forgiveness is more than a leaving behind of blame; it constitutes a healing of the one who forgives. If we find forgiveness difficult than this signifies that the past retains its hold over us. Some people find forgiveness in particular areas very difficult. The things we find difficult to forgive tell us about the people we are. If we find forgiveness difficult for the person who has borrowed money but not returned it, then this signifies that we are perhaps overly concerned about the material aspects of life; perhaps we are threatened by this attack on our physical existence. Another person might find it difficult to forgive a marital cheat. (You can forgive a cheat but you may choose not to live with them). Such a person might themselves be insecure or perhaps have anxieties about their own sexual identity

We are all travelling our own path and along that journey we shall all from time to time encounter many people who will hurt us, who will shatter our expectations, who will destroy our hopes and dreams. And yet, at each and every turn in the road we must remain open to new experiences, new people, new challenges. For if we fail to forgive we carry around with us such a burden of anger and resentment that it becomes impossible to prevent these new events and opportunities being tinged by the flavours of the old.

How can you test whether you have truly forgiven ? You can choose your own test but it is often sufficient to visualise yourself in conversation with the other person. How do you feel in that situation? If you feel angry or upset then you are still clinging to the past. Sometimes it helps to focus your attention not on the negative aspects of what you remember, but the positive aspects. Perhaps your absent or uncaring parents have caused you to become self-reliant, or perhaps being mugged has caused you to become proficient at a martial art.

One warm, generous, open hearted woman found it difficult to forgive her father for cheating on her mother and the traumatic separation that she suffered as a child. Even as an adult she was hardly able to speak to him and could not address him as 'Dad'. Her father had certainly cheated, but he did have other qualities that could not be ignored - he was in some ways a compassionate caring man. I asked her to address the positive qualities that he now expressed, not the old qualities that she remembered, and to forgive him. Concentrating on his positive qualities she re-established a relationship with him, and after a while found it natural to call him 'Dad' again after a space of ten years. Forgiveness is therefore a process of correcting our perception; healing the way in which we perceive the world.

LEAVING THE PAST BEHIND

Forgiveness is also about leaving a part of our past behind. Our personal and spiritual development demands that we let go the rigid beliefs of our past which limit our abilities and perceptions and address the present moment. Removing from our consciousness the garbage that we have brought with us from the past does not necessarily mean leaving behind our home, our family and children - though occasionally this does indeed happen. It has to do with leaving behind only that part of ourselves that is limited by past events, and by feelings that are no longer appropriate to the present. In the words of Kahlil Gibran (The Prophet):

"How shall I go in peace and without sorrow ? Nay, not without a wound in the spirit shall I leave this city. Long were the days of pain I have spent within its walls, and long were the nights of aloneness; and who can depart from his pain without regret ?"

It is a peculiarity of human nature that we often find it difficult to leave behind pain and suffering, to leave behind even our painful past. On the face of it, this is absurd. I think the reason for it lies in the fact that we have invested so much energy, so much commitment to cope with the painful circumstances that it is the very strength of that energy and resolve that makes it difficult for us to escape from them. It is the very strength of our will, the intensity of our focus that now works against us. It is the clenched fist of focus that has become locked tight; we need to release that focus and allow our hand to relax so as to usher in the open palm.

Personal mastery is not necessarily demonstrated by the creation of large or complex structures or vast wealth. Unless those structures and that wealth are precise formulations of our will at the present moment they may act as a snare, a break, a hindrance or a diversionary rather than a liberating influence - a Maginot Line - full of seeming strength but in reality rigid and inflexible, and easily outflanked by changing circumstances.

Personal mastery and power does not lie in the acquisition of followers, the formulation of an all embracing system or the oppression of others. Such power lies in freedom of action; in the freedom to respond creatively and innovatively to new stimuli. Power lies in the freedom to act without the need to overcome mental, emotional or financial inertia. If, therefore, we create for ourselves a lifestyle that commits us to a certain method of functioning, a certain job, or a certain level of income then that which we have created becomes our master, not our servant.

If in our desire to gratify and support our egos we borrow money to support our need for conspicuous consumption then those debts impose control over how we live. We demonstrate the trappings of success but hide the cost in terms of our loss of freedom even from ourselves. We have a tiger by the tail. To tread the world lightly is to draw off only that which we can employ directly in our own lives. It is, wherever possible, to avoid debt. It is to walk through life creating what we need shining fearlessly the light from the beacon of our clearest intent, leaving behind each step no more than a soft imprint of our passing.

Our world has evolved over the years several characteristic social structures to allocate scarce economic resources; the principle one of these being the mechanism of the market, which is self regulating, ruthless in its fairness and implacable in its operation. But running alongside the market is invariably a political structure which often controls about 50% or more of the economic power. These two structures impose an extensive and interlocking web of economic control over virtually all citizens. Only those who are disaffected, who are alienated, who are very wealthy, who ignore the law or who are spiritual warriors are free to some degree from such control.

It is the spiritual warrior's task to live in the world but not to become a part of these structures. To be in the world but not of it. He lives according to his own code. He learns to softly sideslip through the loopholes in the rules leaving a footprint so light that the economic and political structures are powerless; powerless because the warrior is unnoticeable, too silent, too free, too quick for their bureaucracies to register concern over him. Or just maybe too wealthy, too wise, too successful to confront.

An American Sociologist R K Merton once devised a typology of deviance by categorising citizens according to whether or not they personally accepted the goals which society generally regards as desirable, and whether such citizens personally accepted society's prescribed means of obtaining those goals. Those who accepted society's goals but who rejected the approved means of obtaining those goals were the criminal innovators who would employ any and all means available to achieve the financial and social status bought by money. In sharp contrast were those he termed the bureaucratic virtuoso's - people who so completely accepted the approved means of obtaining society's defined goals that they lost sight of the goals themselves. For them, work was primarily a ritual.

Then there were those who had rejected both the goals and the means of obtaining the goals that society prescribes. Into this category fall the tramps and the hermits and all those whose aspirational and workaday commitment to society is weak. The spiritual warrior also falls into this category. His goals are certainly not prescribed by society though he may exhibit coincidentally some of its trappings of success. Likewise, he avoids those means of achieving goals which lock him into a role defined by society. He strives to remain free whilst employing social life and the economy as the tools he has no option but to use. Therefore, no matter what his profession or occupation that working

The spiritual warrior has learned to disassociate himself from the hooks and snares that the world offers to catch him. The average man is available to the world whenever it seeks to clutch him. The warrior learns to be available to the world and unavailable to the world as a matter of choice. Being unavailable involves trusting in the process that carries us forward, having confidence in the universe that it will provide for our needs rather than being compelled to hoard in fear of famine. It involves not worrying; to worry is to become accessible to the world. Being unavailable except by choice involves the creation of a certain detachment from the demands of others. Your availability is signaled by where you place yourself. If you place yourself in the middle of a highway then you signal your availability. If you place yourself carefully in the verge in the shadow of the hedgerow then you signal your detachment.

MY WORD IS LAW

The second most powerful word in any human language is the word 'NO'. It is a word that many people are frightened to use but when used with the force of our will it has the power to overthrow tyrants, oppose intimidators and even deflect photocopier salespeople!

The word 'No' is a vital weapon in your armoury. Without it you cannot but dissipate your energy ineffectively in attempting to deploy it over too many fronts; in half hearted attempts to fulfil the expectations of others. As your focus becomes clearer and more defined so will your use of the word 'No' increase accordingly.

As you acquire focus and learn to employ the English language accurately to describe what you think, feel, and do, the word 'YES' will become the most powerful word in the language to you. The word 'yes' signifies commitment - not just the average man's understanding of the word, but the warrior's. You will use the word 'yes' sparingly because its employment implies the commitment of all and any resources - perhaps ultimately a life and death decision.

We learn to dispense with the cop-out phrases like "I will try" or "I'll see what I can do". Instead there is either simple affirmation or simple denial.

When we say yes with the unbending power of our commitment behind it we are also sending out a powerful affirmation - an affirmation which confirms that we already have all the resources we need to achieve the required result - for otherwise how could we commit ?

The therapeutic practice of Kinesiology recognises the power of words to affect our bodies. If we are muscle tested whilst we repeat the word 'yes' our bodies are strong, gearing up for the anticipated action which is implied by the affirming, committing word. When we repeat the word 'no' we muscle test as weak; our bodies unprepared for action.

For those who have personal power, truth becomes a natural part of their lives. Unafraid of its consequences, they are often viewed as insensitive. But lies, false modesty, manipulation and creeping are the stock in trade of the powerless. The fearful employ deception as a tool, avoid confrontations and seek popularity. Those with personal power are unconcerned with popularity and experience confrontation as just one category of event. Not always pleasant, perhaps, but part of life's rich tapestry nonetheless.

Our words are law when our thoughts, our words, our body language and our actions are all congruent - when every aspect of ourselves gives out the same message. When we lie, when we are unsure of ourselves our bodies betray us by giving out a message which conflicts with the message given out by the spoken word. And this insincerity is often apparent. We probably do not even consciously recognise these body signals for what they are - we maybe just feel that we somehow don't really trust the person who is speaking.

As we gain in personal power our lack of fear for the consequences of our actions and our statements allows us to become increasingly truthful. Our body language and the words we use give out the same message - we become congruent. And as we grow in congruence we become   powerful communicators - able to inspire others and obtain their co-operation. Your word truly becomes Law.

CHAPTER
4

POWER BUILDING TECHNOLOGIES

THE POWER OF BELIEF

Our beliefs are the platform upon which we build our personal power. If the beliefs we have about ourselves are beliefs which do not underpin and sustain the tasks we set for ourselves or the challenges we face then our actions will lack the commitment and energy needed to be successful. Therefore our beliefs can often be our biggest obstacle or our greatest asset. If we have been led to believe that we are powerless, worthless, insignificant then those beliefs can have enormous power to adversely affect our lives. And yet, precisely because those beliefs are ultimately just thoughts and feelings and not physical impediments, they can be changed, in the right circumstances, with amazing speed and ease. Fundamental change in a person can take place literally in the blink of an eye - just as quickly as it takes to change a belief.

Some of my most personally fulfiling work involves changing peoples beliefs about who they are and what they are capable of. It is so satisfying to watch people within the space of a few hours go hurtling through personal barriers, blasting right through the self imposed limitations created and sustained by their beliefs. Suddenly, the world becomes full of opportunity and excitement as the barriers fall away. Lives are changed for ever. Two or three years ago I presented a firewalk in Newton Abbott, Devon. One of the participants was a young man who as a child had been trapped in a burning building. He had lost several fingers in the fire. He chose to confront his fears by doing the firewalk and I was later told that his life had been dramatically changed as a result. His commitment to confront the source of his greatest fear was liberating because no other fears could thereafter have any limiting impact on him.

Beliefs are the framework on which we hang our personal reality. If we believe the world is a threatening place, full of anger and hostility then we interpret our moment to moment experiences in terms of that belief. What we see and personally experience is that world full of anger and hostility. Have you not noticed how some people seem to attract violence ? A belief that the world is a violent, threatening place will inevitably bring forth that experience. An acquaintance of mine experiences violent incidents quite regularly. Now this is not a young man bristling with the arrogance of youth and desperate to demonstrate his machismo in a gang based culture. He's a clever, middle aged man with a good income, notable for his command of languages and his willingness to take offence and to feel threatened in all of them.

If we believe we are capable of carrying out a task then we surely accomplish it effectively. If we believe the task is too much for us then we surely fail in carrying it out. Our beliefs determine our actions; our beliefs invoke our energy or our lethargy. If we believe we can achieve we are correct; if we believe we cannot achieve then we are also correct. Knowing this it follows that certain beliefs are intrinsically more valuable; more empowering; more financially rewarding than others. Likewise some beliefs contribute to our physical, emotional and mental well being and stability; others are limiting, emotionally distressing and destabilizing.

I list below a few beliefs which are intrinsically empowering and energising. These beliefs are so powerful that it does not matter over-much whether at the outset you truly accept these beliefs. If you adopt and employ these beliefs as if they were true to you, they will very quickly take root in your subconscious and produce the same effect. Your as if actions act as a powerful affirmation that can break through the limitations imposed on you by your present beliefs. They also affirm that it is your choice to believe whatever you wish - and affirming your power to choose is, as discussed earlier, the first step on the path to empowerment.

1. *Everything has a purpose and that purpose serves me*
This belief recognises and affirms that the universe exists as an extension of ourselves; that no matter what we encounter there is always in the end a positive and fruitful outcome - our growth. And that growth is nearly always accompanied by growing pains as we stretch and strive to handle new feelings.

2. *There is no such thing as failure - only feedback*
Without this belief there would be very few discoveries. Only by being persistent, by suffering sometimes many apparent 'failures' and setbacks do we learn of the multiplicity of 'wrong' ways to attempt a task. Each 'failure' in reality takes us closer to ultimate success. Each 'failure' is a stepping stone toward success. Every successful salesman intellectually knows and emotionally accepts this belief.

3. *I take responsibility for everything I am, for everything I do*
This belief is an affirmation of your personal power; it declares that you acknowledge as your own all that you are, all that you do. It acknowledges and affirms that you stand accountable for yourself and for your actions.

4. *My Word is Law*
When you internalise this belief you are a living expression of your commitment to the principles outlined in this book. Your word has become your bond. You choose to give it, to withhold it or to express your silence on the matter. What you do not do is to mislead.

52 There are many more beliefs that can be usefully adopted. The above are for me the most empowering and the most useful.

THE POWER OF BREATH

Breath sustains life. It is our primary means of interacting with the world about us - all other methods are intermittent. With breathing we have to make a conscious effort to stop the process and until death we are able to halt the interaction only for a short time. Breathing is the source of the life force sometimes called prana or breath energy. When we breathe in we take in oxygen and when we breathe out we exhale carbon dioxide. We have two lungs, the right and the left each with compartments stacked vertically. The lower compartments of each lung hardly get used at all in the commonly experienced shallow breathing that the majority of people employ most of the time.

Of course, most people take in sufficient oxygen to sustain life, but they do not know how to breathe efficiently, so as to gather in the pranic energy. To do this is not difficult. We simply need to draw our breath into the belly region of our bodies. This is called diaphramatic or belly breathing, and uses all the compartments of our lungs.

To do this we must be relaxed and not worry too much about letting our bellies sag. Breathe in gently but deeply, allowing the belly region to inflate first and keeping the chest uninflated. As the belly inflates it first expands and then, when full, it flattens once again as the chest inflates and it, in turn, expands.

For some people this type of breathing at first seems highly stylised but after just a few days practice you will find that it becomes the natural way for you to breathe. If you set aside a time twice a day to do this belly breathing with as little as 15 breaths on each occasion, you will find that within a month you will experience a distinct change in your energy level. Developing this natural deep pattern of breathing is a fundamental step toward strengthening your immune system and the acquisition of pranic energy

Some people, especially the middle aged and elderly who have not taken regular exercise, may find at first that they feel light headed and giddy when they first try out this method of breathing. This is simply because their bodies are unused to the increased supply of oxygen and a little time is needed for adjustment. Before I started breathing exercises I had great difficulty in blowing up balloons. Before you start your breathing exercises see how well you cope with this task. Within a month or two you will be absolutely amazed by the difference. I discovered that after only two or three weeks practice I could blow up balloons effortlessly, virtually bursting a balloon with a single breath.

Merely be taking in a greater volume of oxygen through the practice of belly breathing we can dramatically improve the body's ability to heal itself. Professional football team managers employ hyperbaric or oxygen therapy to reduce the recovery time for injured players at a cost of £35,000 - £40,000 for each unit. When skipper Paul McStay of Celtic tore medial knee ligaments his club became the very first to employ the therapy. He was expected to be out of action for at least four months, but with the aid of the therapy he was back playing in half that time.

EXERCISES

1. GREETING THE SUN

Stand with your legs slightly apart and with your arms loosely by your sides. As you slowly inhale bring your hands upwards and inwards until the fingers of each hand meet in front of your belly with the palms upward. As you continue inhaling let your hands continue upward until your arms are outstretched above your head, letting your hands naturally twist so that your palms face upward at the fullest reach of your arms. As you begin to exhale bring your arms down in a wide arc on each side of your body until your arms are by your side once more. Adjust the speed of your movement so that your inhale finishes with your arms fully outstretched above your head, and your exhale finishes with your arms by your sides. Your breath should be slow, deep and natural. Repeat 15 times.

When you are comfortable with this basic form you can begin adding

54   the following enhancements:

(a) When your hands reach the outstretched position above your head hold your position and your breath for, say, a count of six or for whatever higher or lower number is comfortable for you

(b) When you reach the position with your arms by your sides ensure that you are as completely as possible exhaled and then hold for a count of six or for whatever higher or lower number is comfortable for you

(c) As you inhale rise up onto your toes; as you exhale sink back down on to your heels

2. RIDING THE HORSE

Stand with your feet wide apart, knees bent, your rear sitting in an imaginary saddle and your feet pointing to the front. Your hands should be clenched into loose fists at your sides, with your elbows sticking out behind you. Discover the width of stance that is right for you by gradually increasing the distance between your feet. This stance is very tiring for the newcomer. Use your willpower to maintain the stance for that little bit longer each day. Hold the position for as long as you wish. Your breath should be slow deep and natural. It is unnecessary to count individual breaths. As you gain in proficiency you will find it easy to go lower. Try working up to holding the stance for five to ten minutes at a time over a period of two or three months.

3. HOLDING THE BALLOON

Take up a stance similar to the Riding Horse stance but not so exaggerated. Your feet should be a little closer together, your knees not quite so bent. Your arms, instead of being at your sides, should be held out naturally in front of you bent at the elbows with palms facing inwards as if holding a very large spherical balloon. As you breathe in move your arms outward as if your breath inflates the balloon. As you breath out move your arms inward as if the balloon is deflating. Remember to breath in and out slowly and deeply, with rhythm. Do this exercise 16 times, counting each inhale and exhale as one. As you gain confidence hold your breath when the balloon is fully inflated for a count of six (or such lower number as you feel comfortable with). Hold the exhale position for a similar number.

THE POWER OF FOOD

Actually, it doesn't seem to matter overmuch what we eat provided we do everything else that we ought to do to keep our bodies fit and healthy. If we have a vigorous physical lifestyle it seems to matter not at all what we eat. The diet of the Inuit or Eskimo is a total overload of cholesterol but their bodies work without complaint. Our difficulty lies in the fact that our lives are no longer physical. Most of us take insufficient exercise and with our increasingly sedentary lifestyle what we eat becomes increasingly important.

And a lot of nonsense is talked about food. Some very expensive protein mixtures are imported from the USA and networked in the UK. It does not take a brain the size of a planet to know that protein is body building food and carbohydrate is energy providing food. And yet I am regularly encouraged by the purveyors of these mixtures that I should buy some of this protein rich food because of its excellent energy producing qualities. The truth is exactly the opposite.

In fact, nearly all of us eat too much protein. Mother's milk at birth contains 2.4% protein reducing to 1.5% after six months. Since it is as babies that we grow fastest and therefore require the maximum amount of protein, it follows that any diet which provides more than 1.5% protein has got its numbers wrong. Excess protein intake produces excess nitrogen which causes fatigue and reduces stamina. Too much protein has also been linked with osteoporosis - the softening and weakening of the bones. Now, I am not an expert on nutrition, but it seems to me that the lesson given to us by nature in the form of mother's milk is exceedingly clear. Cut down on your protein intake until it represents no more than 2% of your diet.

For those who are considering going vegetarian but are concerned about the difficulty of obtaining sufficient protein from a vegetarian diet, I hope that the preceding remarks will give them some comfort. A vegetarian diet is actually healthier than a meat eaters diet. Meat contains a high level or uric acid - one of the body's waste products - which if not quickly removed from the blood can cause gout and bladder stones. The body is capable of eliminating in a day only about half the amount of uric acid found in an average sized portion of meat, so give your refuse disposal system a hand and cut down or eliminate your meat intake.

Those who practice bodybuilding regularly take in excess protein and consequently they have very little stamina. A person taking an average amount of exercise with a low protein diet probably has more stamina than the average TV gladiator. Take the gorilla. In terms of muscle bulk and body weight the gorilla outstrips the strongest and most enthusiastic bodybuilder and yet the gorilla is totally reliant on a fruit and vegetable diet. Another lesson for those who wish to cultivate the body beautiful.

Humans, like gorillas, are primates, a family of mammals who forage for food. Some primates do eat meat but in their natural environment it is mainly vegetable matter that is consumed. We are very different from the large carnivores who live exclusively on meat and who eat irregularly. Our bodies and minds work best when given the type of food for which they appear to be designed - bulky, water-rich foods in the form of fruit and vegetables.

Fruit is digested not in our stomach, but in the large intestine. It therefore makes sense to eat fruit only on an empty stomach or after having previously eaten fruit. If we follow this rule then the fruit we eat will not get held up on top of the food in our stomach and ferment creating large volumes of gas.

Certain foods are digested in an acidic digestive medium, others in an alkaline medium. If therefore we eat foods requiring different digestive mediums at the same time they will take a very long time to be digested and for the waste products to be passed out of our system. These considerations give us some Food Rules:

1 Do not eat high protein foods (meat, cheese, fish, eggs, milk)
   with high carbohydrate foods (bread, beans, cereals, potatoes)
2. Do not eat high protein foods with fatty foods
3. Do not eat fruit with or after any other food
4. Eat high protein foods with vegetables
5. Eat high carbohydrate foods with vegetables
6. Only drink before a meal, never during or after. Drinking
   with a meal dilutes the digestive juices and delays digestion.
7. Drink more water

About 60% of our body is water. As we age our natural thirst mechanism does not work so efficiently and by the time we feel thirsty we are already dehydrated. Your urine should be a pale straw colour. If it is any darker than this you are dehydrated.

When our bodies are properly hydrated they work at peak efficiency. Before walking on broken glass I always top up my body with a litre of water. Proper hydration enables the body to get rid of waste products more easily and stops us getting tired, impatient or irritable - all symptoms of dehydration

The amount and type of food we eat reflects our life. When we carry excess weight it can indicate that our lives have become stuck, our growth impeded. We are focusing on food as a provider of security; as food for our ego. When the pounds begin to fall off it is often an indication that the pace of our lives has changed; we no longer need to placate the demands of our ego and we are ready to strike out into the big wide world which has suddenly become exciting rather than frightening. When I got stuck in an unsatisfactory marriage my weight ballooned to a massive sixteen and a half stone. Within four months of confronting the issues involved and choosing to leave my then wife my weight dropped to thirteen and a half stone. Is your weight an indicator of the degree to which you are 'stuck' ?

The body, like the mind, needs work, discipline and practice if it is to reach its full potential and to remain a healthy efficient system. If we make no demands on our bodies then our muscles atrophy and our defense mechanisms lose their effectiveness. In order to live a long, powerful and effective life we need to exercise our bodies regularly.

In the past much exercise was obtained in the normal course of going about one's daily life. We would hunt, gather, cultivate and escape from predators all of which would involve the use of our bodies. Today we lead sedentary lives and it requires most of us to make a special effort in order to take the regular exercise that our bodies' need.

The body is the vehicle that provides the means for our spirit to express itself in the physical plane. There is no other means. To honour that importance we must pay attention to its needs and also we must exert sufficient authority over it for it to become a powerful and effective instrument of our will.

Muscle Tone - Bodies that are not worked lose muscle tone. They become flabby; they atrophy and increasingly are unable to respond effectively to physical demands. After a while physical demands are avoided because of the effort and a vicious circle of avoidance and physical inactivity results.

Lymphatic System - The body's key defense mechanism is the lymphatic system which is a network extending throughout the body containing a clear fluid called lymph. This fluid is not moved about our bodies by a pump like the heart but by muscular movement. If therefore we take little or no exercise then our muscles are unused and our lymphatic system becomes ineffective and we develop a weak immune system.

We can never completely avoid coming into contact with bacteria and disease if we wish to live a normal life. And even if we choose to isolate ourselves from others there are still many bugs that are always with us; it is only the power of our immune system which prevents them from affecting us. The bug that causes pneumonia, for example, is always in our bodies but it is only when our immune system is weak that it actually attacks us. Likewise, we all produce cancerous cells but it is only the weakness of our immune system and its inability to identify and destroy those malignant cells that allows us to actually contract the disease. Helping to maintain a healthy immune system through moderate exercise is therefore a must.

Stress - Excess stress diminishes the effectiveness of our immune system. Stress is experienced whenever we encounter an experience which we find threatening. When faced by such a threat the body responds by feeding into the bloodstream a chemical cocktail enabling the body to fight against or flee from the threat with utmost efficiency. But today such a simplistic biological response is almost always inappropriate. Consequently the chemical cocktail in our bloodstream is not dispersed by the violent physical exercise involved in fighting or fleeing, and we therefore tend to remain in a constant state of semi-arousal, with a chemical overload stuck in our bloodstream. Clearly, one way of reducing that persistent stress level is to take hard physical exercise which has the effect of burning off the chemicals in our blood stream.

Bone Density - Walking and running - exercises which involve the weight of our bodies impacting on the ground - can help prevent osteoporosis, the weakening of the bones. Whilst generally good, swimming will not help in this regard

The Heart - Exercises that stimulate heart and lung activity for sufficiently long to produce beneficial changes in the body are termed aerobic exercises. Running, swimming, cycling, jogging are all good for this purpose. An aerobic exercise program is designed to steadily increase the ability of the body to process oxygen and in doing so improves lung capacity and creates a powerful heart. Aerobic capacity is the best measure of physical fitness.

The very best book to buy on aerobics is 'The New Aerobics' written by Kenneth H Cooper and published by Bantam. The author developed the official exercise program for the US Air Force and Navy and the

Royal Canadian Air Force. The book was first published some years ago but to me is the definitive work on the subject.

THE POWER OF MEDITATION

There are numerous mental exercises which are described as meditation. They all have in common what they set out to do - to slow down the frequency of our brain waves from the usual frequency of between 14 and 30 cycles per second (the Beta state) to a frequency of between 7 and 14 cycles per second (the Alpha state). In very deep meditation we reach the Theta state, which is characterised by brain wave activity of between 4 and 7 cycles per second.

The Alpha state represents a slightly altered state of consciousness where our ego's are less dominant. In this state our minds can experience a particularly pure form of consciousness because we are temporarily freed from the emotions and limitations of our own personal perspective; our perceptions freed from the need to judge. We are also able to experience more subtle, delicate sensations normally hidden from us. We also feel very calm, clear headed and relaxed.

Breathing Rate - In 1965 Dr. John Allison measured the rate of breathing of meditators and found that it changed from the usual 12 or so breaths per minute to an average of 6 breaths per minute. More startling was the fact that these six breaths were so shallow as to be hardly detectable. A respiratory physiologist estimated that a drop in metabolic rate of 75% had occurred and commented that the subjects should, by all accounts, be dead !

Blood Pressure - In 1976 Dr Robert Keith Wallace in America confirmed that meditators consumed less oxygen. At the same time as the reduction in breathing there was a reduction in heart rate and blood pressure.

Effect on Aging - In 1978 Dr Wallace researched the effects of meditation on the aging process. He measured the biological ages of meditators and compared them with the biological ages of the general population. He discovered that meditators were significantly younger biologically than their same aged counterparts who did not meditate, and the longer a person had meditated the greater the difference between their chronological age and their biological age.

A further study suggested that every year of meditation takes off roughly one year of biological aging. Then in 1980, in a landmark study, Harvard psychologist Charles Alexander went into three old peoples homes and taught sixty of the residents (all at least 80 years old) three techniques - relaxation, mind sharpening games and meditation. Each person only learned one technique. Three years later when Alexander returned to the old age homes about one third of the residents had died, including 24% of those who had not learned meditation. But for the group who had learned meditation the death rate was zero!

Tuning Out - The meditative of Alpha state may be regarded as a state in which we have succeeded in tuning out the numerous disruptive influences that normally affect us. There is a method of achieving this that I think may be common to all meditation techniques. First the attention is diverted away from distracting thoughts and then secondly the mind is occupied by another simple thought pattern or activity which is capable of being carried on without tension. Since this new thought pattern or activity requires very little physical or mental energy to sustain it, the mind naturally relaxes into the Alpha state. Precisely because there is this tuning out aspect to meditation we find that meditating for about 20 minutes can be extraordinarily restful.

Meditation Techniques: There are two main techniques which are very simple to learn and which are very effective right from the start:

(1) Counting Breaths - Sit comfortably in an upright chair or cross legged with your back straight. Leaning against a wall is fine. Close your eyes and start silently to count your breaths - counting an inhale and an exhale as a count of one. Breath into your belly as described previously, slowly and rhythmically until you reach a count of 10. Then restart the count at 1 again. If you lose track of your count or your mind drifts off to concern itself with your usual day to day concerns simply return to the count starting at the beginning again. This will inevitably happen to you

frequently. But as you continue counting you will observe that your breathing slows down, and as it slows down you may notice that there will be moments when you have neither counted nor had thoughts - when you have been a pure observer. At first you will fill in these gaps almost immediately with your thoughts, but with continued practice and as your breathing slows down further you will find that the gap between your breaths expands and will increasingly be left free from thought. You will be experiencing pure consciousness - consciousness unadulterated by thought.

(2)   Using a Mantra - Sit yourself down with your eyes closed as in the previous method but instead of counting your breaths repeat to yourself silently a word that has no meaning - at least no meaning that you are aware of - e.g. nomadew, krospin etc. Again, if your mind drifts off simply remind yourself gently to continue the repetition of the nonsense word (the mantra). After a while your breathing will slow down and with practice, in the gap between each repetition of the mantra, there will arise the pure consciousness described in the previous method. You can also use mantras which do have a meaning to you - such as AUM.

These two methods are I believe the two simplest methods to work with. The second method is the method used by those who practice Transcendental Meditation, though in that system the teacher prescribes a certain mantra to the student based upon the student's age. Whichever method you choose to use - and no one was ever harmed by using both methods - you should try to practice twice a day for between 20 and 45 minutes on each occasion. If you have a demanding job and you find that you arrive home feeling stressed out you should get into the habit of doing your meditation session before you do anything else at all. By getting into the habit of regular meditation and relying on its ability to eliminate stress you will be sending a message to your body and your subconscious that you are empowered to heal and nurture yourself.

If you are having to survive on less sleep than you would like, then use 20 minutes meditation and 10 minutes Reiki (see later in this book) to revitalise yourself.

As you become more proficient at meditating you will find that you come to recognise the meditative state easily, and you will be able increasingly to access that state almost immediately you have the desire. You can encourage this process by creating for yourself one or more useful triggers that you and your body associate with the meditative state. For me, merely sitting cross legged with my back straight up against a wall acts as a powerful trigger.

What you don't want to happen when you meditate is to get interruptions. You should tell your partner and/or your children to leave you alone, and unplug the telephone. Avoid meditating immediately after a meal or with a full stomach. Wear comfortable clothes and loose fitting shoes or take your shoes off.

Meditation can have a profound effect on your health and general well-being. Let it become part of your life.

THE POWER OF EMOTION

Emotions are associated with and can express both profound joy and profound pain. They are the storms, the winds and the peaceful sunsets which cross the oceans, the flux between our physical and mental bodies. They represent the turbulence, the cavitation created by our energy and the bow wave created by our movement as we cut through the water of life.

Many books and people are united in the view that we should always give free vent to our emotions, rather than stifle, repress and hide them. For if we fail to express our emotions it is said that we interfere with an entirely natural process; we create blocks in the free flow of energy within us. But this view is far too simplistic. Those who give fully of their emotions, those who are emotional by nature are, in my experience, people who lack stamina, who are quickly exhausted by the storms of feeling that rage through their bodies. Their energy drains away and they are left with insufficient energy to mobilise their resources. In fact it is our emotions which are generally the biggest drain on our energy. When we always give free vent to our emotions, when we give out full throttle emotional energy over every trifling irritation then we have a major energy leakage; we are out of control, and dissipating our energy ineffectively. It is a question of being able to employ our emotions or have them employ us. The warrior needs to be able to feel emotion but not necessarily to be persuaded by it. Should the tail wag the dog ?

If, however, we learn to express our emotions in a conscious deployment of energy and with an intensity that is appropriate to the importance of the subject, then our feelings become a part of the power that we employ in expressing our will and our emotions become a wise and effective use of our energy. Therefore we must strive to acquire an element of detachment from the experiences we encounter. This detachment arises as we acquire that inner peace borne of a strategic viewpoint and a trust in our transcendent nature.

Thus we must learn to exert a degree of control over our emotions; to focus and use them in the same way as we learn to focus and use our other resources. And before we object too quickly to this awful idea of stifling or controlling our emotions let us first understand that in reality we already choose to a large degree the emotions we experience, because what we feel is determined by what we believe; by the way in which we interpret our experiences. Merely by holding fast to a few empowering beliefs, by taking a more strategic viewpoint - one not swayed by day to day difficulties, by practicing the old fashioned positive thinking, we can relatively easily break the stranglehold that our emotions may have over us. Instead, our emotions can become another powerful asset in our personal and spiritual armoury.

There is a widely respected discipline - neuro linguistic programming (NLP) which is based on the premise that we can choose the mental state that we wish to have. Although I am not personally attracted to NLP because I feel it imposes yet another layer of programming on the individual, I mention it here merely to evidence the fact that there are in fact many people out there who are saying that you don't have to be a slave to your emotions.

Employing our emotions as a positive asset is very different from

simply exerting a rigid control over them - bottling them up and seeking
to give the impression that our emotions are other than as we portray
them. Clint Eastwood in those wonderful Spaghetti Westerns provided
the stereotype for that behaviour. As the Man with No Name his face was
an expressionless mask. In the real world people who have this rigid grip
on their emotions are those who are actually frightened to reveal
themselves; who feel unworthy to show their inner selves. Instead, they
may, perhaps as a compensating quality, develop the ability to focus their
attention irrespective of their emotions. This is not an unworthy quality
in itself, but, as with all good qualities if used to excess and without
balance and perspective it becomes counterproductive. Furthermore,
those who are locked into this type of response are quite unable to call
on the full flood of their power which is available when all resources -
including emotions - are working in concert.

Those who, like the Man with No Name, have buttoned down their
emotions have a difficult task ahead. They must first unlearn the
rigidity they have learned over perhaps many years. With little effective
emotional interaction and experience to sustain them they are
emotionally immature. They lack the confidence to express emotion or
the depth to sustain relationships. It is likely that they have passed
through numerous unsatisfactory relationships in their quest for
emotional sustenance.

The spiritual warrior, in his freedom from the imperative demands of
fear; in the confidence of his or her own unique worth, is free to give full
vent to his or her emotions. Yet, because of that confidence, that
personal power and strategic viewpoint or sense of detachment his or
her immediate need to express emotion is diminished. The warrior
therefore rests in watchful peacefulness until the time for action and the
time for emotion is considered desirable.

That action may simply be to express emotion as an end in itself - to
release the pressure of emotion that he notices within, or, for example,
perhaps to give full emotional expression to his feelings for his partner
or to experience in full his sorrow in a bereavement. He does this not for

reassurance or justification or to share responsibility, but to bring himself back into balance.

Alternatively the warrior master may use his emotions, his tears or his joyfulness as a tribute, an offering to another or perhaps as a tool to inspire or to spur on others by the expression of his congruence and intensity of feeling. That these emotions are conscious and directed does not mean they are contrived. Neither are they the false emotions that an actor portrays. The only difference lies in the degree of consciousness or self observation employed by the master.

On the road to becoming warriors let us learn to notice and be aware of our emotions as they flow through us. They are the signposts, the calls to action and the feedback we receive. Let us notice these signals and choose to live rather than driven by them. Let us choose to amend our habitual, mechanical, modes of response and create for ourselves new innovative responses which preserve and enhance our freedom.

THE POWER OF THOUGHT

Much has been written and spoken about the power of positive thinking. It has become a cliché for those in the personal development movement. In essence, positive thinking is no more than having a positive or optimistic expectation about the future.

Negative Expectations : If we have a negative expectation about our abilities or the outcome of an event then we make no effort to achieve; we are unable to summon our energy, we simply don't try. 'What's the use ?' we say. If on the other hand we have a positive expectation then we make an effort to achieve the goal that we see as within our grasp. We easily focus our energy to reach out and achieve what we desire. The lesson is therefore clear. Whether you believe or you disbelieve you can achieve a certain goal, in each case you are correct. Your expectations are self-fulfiling. If therefore you wish to attain success, if you wish to summon your energy to achieve definite goals then it is essential that you have a positive mental attitude.

Many people exhibit negativity; they blame others, they assert their own powerlessness, they are unwilling to take action, they see themselves as unworthy. Such expectations are then often passed onwards from one generation to another. Even when a parent actually tells a child that he or she has the ability to achieve outstanding success the statement has very limited impact on the child unless the parent exhibits at least some of that positive expectancy about themselves. They must walk their talk if they wish to inspire their son or daughter. As your own positivity increases you become increasingly aware of just how much negativity finds its way into everyday conversation.

Positive Expectations: A high expectation of success is the single most important factor in achieving success. Experiments have been conducted where subjects were given certain tasks to undertake. Some were led to believe that the tasks were very easy, others were told they were very difficult. Those experimental subjects who believed the tasks to be easy consistently achieved better results irrespective of the type of work undertaken. When a child believes that he or she has the ability to succeed then the child will almost certainly live up to those expectations as an adult. Belief is the key. Belief in oneself empowers. Without such belief you have already created the limits of your ability and of your own power.

So how can we become optimistic ? How do we learn to have high expectations about ourselves ? Since our present beliefs have been learned from others and from our experiences to date we have a fair amount of unlearning to do. The best way to unlearn something is to proceed on the principle that good thoughts drive out bad thoughts; that positivity drives out negativity. Therefore don't beat yourself up about every negative thought you have, just concentrate on contradicting it with a positive thought. Give yourself some simple daily practice in affirming your self worth, your ability and competence. Here is an example of an affirmation that you could use. Repeat it daily until it becomes second nature to you; until it or your own affirmations spring into your mind as an automatic response to any remote sniff of negativity:

I am able and competent. I have all the resources I need. I achieve success. I perform well. Difficult tasks are placed before me to stretch me further and help me grow. I am good, honest, loving, compassionate and true

Become aware of your thoughts and the words that you choose to speak and counter each negative thought or word with a positive affirmation. Soon, and with surprisingly little difficulty you will find that you have eradicated your negative thoughts.

Resist Not Negative Suggestions: If someone else expresses their limiting or negative expectations about you remind yourself that you have a choice about whether to accept the suggestion or not. DO NOT enter into a discussion or an argument about the suggestion you have received. To do so would be to give power to the suggestion by treating it as having sufficient merit to warrant argument. In biblical language the message is 'resist not evil'. For once you begin to argue you become focused on the messenger rather than the message you are seeking to deflect. You can deflect limiting suggestions about your competence by saying to yourself:

These words slide past me. My own perception is clear. I am able and competent (continue with above affirmation)

And as you say the affirmation you can visualise the negative words being spoken to you sliding past you diagonally in a slimy dribble.

Negative Thoughts about Others: Yes, some people are indeed easier to love and to have high expectations about than others. But when we allow negative thoughts about people to enter our minds we are encouraging them to fulfil our low expectations. We are also denying ourselves the opportunity to correct our own limited thinking. And that might just be a worthwhile challenge for us. If you catch yourself having negative thoughts about a person say to yourself:

These thoughts slide away from me. My own perception is clear. I see the unlimited capacity and loving nature of this person

As you say these words visualise the negative thoughts sliding away from you diagonally in a slimy dribble.

Always use Positive Affirmations: In other words, don't say to yourself

"He is not incompetent" or "I am not poor" rather you should say "He has ability" or "I have everything I need"

Watch the Results: If you rigorously impose these disciplines on your thinking you will be amazed at the relatively short time it takes to completely change the beliefs you have about yourself and the world. If you have become accustomed to thinking about the world as an unfulfilling, tough place then that indeed is what you are probably experiencing. But if you come to think about the world as a positive and invigorating place then your behaviour will change and that is how you will experience the world. It matters little whether at the outset you consciously believe the affirmations that you employ provided that at the very least you would like to believe in them. Indeed, your disbelief is actually to be expected, for if you truly believed in the affirmations that you use then you would not need to use them! By regularly employing affirmations (good thoughts) you are driving out your limiting and negative thinking (bad thoughts).

What you are doing is correcting your human perception; conducting a healing exercise upon yourself. You are teaching yourself to address not the apparent imperfections that your human eyes see, but rather the infinite and unlimited spirit within - the God force, the divine spark which we all share.

Christian Science and several other religious sects and denominations employ these ideas to effect healings. Students of Christian Science learn to perceive and address men and women in their true unlimited nature - as perfect beings created in the image and likeness of God. Irrespective of the particular merits of Christian Science as a religion, for me there is no doubt that if we learn to relate to people as representatives of the divine then we employ a very powerful healing force.

THE POWER OF REIKI

Reiki is the system of natural healing rediscovered by Dr Mikao Usui in the middle of the last century in Japan. It is unlike any other healing system because a Reiki student's ability to channel the healing energy of

Reiki is switched on almost as quickly and as easily as switching on a light bulb, using a very ancient piece of probably Tibetan spiritual technology. To accomplish this a Reiki Master (the rather grandiose term to describe a person who has reached the third level of Reiki) simply takes the student through a short ritual or ceremony called an attunement. There is no acceptable scientific explanation as to how this phenomenon occurs. It just does, and it is probably the most frequently experienced example of ritual magic at work in the world today.

At the First Degree stage the student normally receives four attunements which have the effect of opening up the physical body to channel the healing energy through to the hands. At the Second Degree stage, usually taken a few months after First Degree, the student usually receives a further two attunements which activate three semi-secret symbols used to manipulate the healing energy. One of these symbols enables the student to undertake absent healing.

At the Third Degree the student receives a further symbol - the Master symbol - which enables him or her to give attunements to others.

Reiki can be used to heal any illness or disease because it works primarily by helping the body's own healing mechanisms to do their job more effectively. In practice, it also operates, where the need arises, as a kind of carrier wave for other forms of spiritual healing where Reiki alone might not offer the greatest chance of success.

Reiki is important, not merely for healing in the regular sense, but more generally as a tool for personal development. Tradition has it that once you have taken Reiki into your life you embark on a journey without previous precedent. In the first two years after taking the First Degree initiations most students lives noticeably change. It is as if the additional energy and cleansing provided by Reiki serves to gently push the student off their existing point of balance, leaving them free to search out and acquire a new balance point at a higher level.

Reiki, especially at the Second Degree, also has the effect of stimulating and opening up the psychic and mediumship abilities of the student. Traditionally it is said to open the Third Eye. In my work as a Reiki

Master I have experienced many astounding instances of this, the most dramatic example being my friend Jill Laidlaw who within a week of receiving her Second Degree attunements became a full blown and very powerful medium.

There is much more that I could write about Reiki but there are already many books written on the subject. Besides, Reiki is not a subject to be studied; it is rather a way of life, a discipline to be practiced and experienced. In fact, I tell my students NOT to buy any books about Reiki, at least in the early stages. To practice Reiki successfully does not require academic ability or intellectual study. The student is empowered by the attunement process to be a channel for the energy which travels automatically to wherever in the recipient the need is greatest.

I thoroughly recommend Reiki to anyone seeking an inexpensive stimulus for their personal growth. Today, if you shop around you will not need to pay more than £60.00 for First Degree and £80.00 - £120.00 for Second Degree. I have recently seen an advertisement for the Third or Masters Degree in Kindred Spirit magazine for £75.00. At these prices Reiki is an absolute bargain. And, if you want pure Reiki uncluttered by personal opinions you will not lose anything by going for these lower cost alternatives.

THE POWER OF SECRECY

Have you noticed how some people talk incessantly about what they intend doing, about what they will achieve, about what great efforts they will make. And is it not usually the case that these very same people have usually achieved nothing six months or a year later ? Every time you talk idly about a project you dissipate whatever energy you have to accomplish it.

When the warrior considers projects and makes plans for the future he assesses the energy available to him to accomplish each task. His inner yearning, his heart, directs his focus and direction and he therefore finds it easy to visualise the end result. He is excited and energised by his vision.

But, knowing how energy is created, managed and dissipated he is cautious, reserved, even secretive about discussing his ideas and plans, even with his closest friends. It is not that he is concerned that his ideas will be stolen; it is simply that he knows that unnecessary chit chat about future action ALWAYS diminishes the energy available to take that action. It becomes a partial substitute for that action; an end in itself. Even in the preliminary stages where he will need to gather information from others he will deal with them on a need-to-know basis. This secrecy serves to bottle up and preserve the energy the warrior creates through his emotion and imagination as he focuses on the project. If you wish to follow the path that your heart yearns for then your progress will be faster if you walk the first few faltering steps in silence.

THE POWER OF COMMUNICATION

Effective communication invariably involves the use of a shared language. Whether we choose to express ourselves in words or by the use of a set of visual symbols those words or symbols take on some of the power that we employ in using them. Take the word freedom. Once upon a time the word was created to express a certain meaning - let us say the absence of repression. But after frequent usage the word acquired a very powerful emotional charge assigned to it by those who used it most   frequently and with the greatest vehemence - those fighting against repression. The word became a rallying cry. But after a while others not directly involved in the creation of freedom, and even those who were actually in the business of repression itself begin to use the word because of the emotional power associated with it, and the political advantage arising from it. Of course, after a while, the word began to lose its emotional power because of this cynical high jacking of its emotional charge. Today in political life it is now impossible to use the word without it sounding like a worn out cliche.

We can choose to give our power to any object or symbol and in doing so our meaning and intent flows through the object which then in turn communicates our vision and power. Take the tarot cards. If you have learned to use the tarot you will probably have realised that the precise meaning that you choose to give a card need not be the same meaning that the instruction book or anyone else tells you it should be. The key lies in your being certain and clear about the meaning that you personally choose to assign each card. Provided that you consistently employ that same meaning every time you encounter that same card your reading will be every bit as good as anyone else's. The same principle holds good when we apply it to communication in general. When we are very clear about the meanings that we assign to the words that we use, and when those meanings are re-inforced by the emotional charge that we assign to them, then the words we employ are powerful communicators of the message that we wish to convey.

When we use our power of choice; when we are firm in our intent and demonstrate that intent by employing ritual, emotion or consistency, then we are able to communicate and transfer our power to others. When we are excited, eager or enthusiastic the quality of our communication changes. We become persuasive. Fairly early on in my career I was a sales representative for an oil company. My job was to visit direct consumers of petroleum products such as haulage contractors in order to persuade them to buy my company's products. It was not a job that I felt comfortable with and my personal and social skills were then undeveloped but I found that my enthusiasm and eagerness, being the youngest person in the company ever to have been appointed to the position, won over many new customers. I even became the UK salesman of the month, despite my lack of social graces.

I often talk about congruence in my workshops. Congruence makes communication incredibly effective, and congruent is generally what we are when we are enthusiastic. Congruence is what occurs when our mind, our thoughts, our emotions and our body language are all saying the same thing; are all giving out the same message. It is actually quite difficult for most people to lie convincingly because when we lie our body language usually betrays us; we appear shifty, implausible, unconvincing. When, however, we communicate in a congruent way we can transfer our energy, our vision and our power to others easily. This is especially significant in personal growth workshops where the facilitator must be able to 'inspire' the participants to go above and beyond their beliefs and expectations about themselves. If the facilitator expresses powerfully and congruently his belief in the ability of the participants, the participants will become empowered to fulfil the facilitators high expectations rather than their own mediocre beliefs.

When we lie or express ourselves incongruently we communicate confusing messages to our own psyche; our bodies and to others. There is an internal pressure on us not to lie but because of our fears most people choose to redefine their reality so that the reality becomes consonant with their lies. I am not a thief, we say; I merely took what was due to me because the person from whom we took the articles was so selfish/arrogant/rude etc etc. Of course, once this happens our whole perceptual apparatus becomes faulty.

Communicating truthfully involves being true to our truth, not adulterating it or watering it down for mass consumption. Often this means we will be perceived as rude and unfeeling. When I practiced as a conveyancer I worked primarily in the field of domestic conveyancing - doing the legal work for people moving house. For most people moving house is quite stressful, and when things go wrong or even if things go even very slightly amiss in terms of timing the client tends to make emotional demands on the person doing the legal work. Having done the job for many years one develops a sense of when it is necessary and productive to apply pressure and when it pointless; when it is appropriate to take action and when it is not. Clients have not developed this sense and therefore tend to create problems with their emotionally charged attempts at clearing delays. My way of dealing with clients at such points has always been to state facts clearly and unemotionally but with little or no attempt to provide emotional support. Rightly or wrongly it never seemed to me to be part of my job to do that and consequently word would get back to me from time to time about how rude and unhelpful I had been. I, on the other hand, would recall the conversation as one in which I had merely related the facts, leaving it to the client to themselves come to terms with the situation.

As a student I worked for a while with Oleg Cannon, the son of the one time well known Electrical Trades Union leader, in the Large Toys Department at Bentalls the department store in Kingston Upon Thames, where we worked as temporary staff over the Christmas period. Intending customers would seek our advice about what large toy to buy their children. As young men hired temporarily to cope with the Christmas spending spree we were really not ourselves very interested in large toys and in any event knew even less than our customers about what their children would like. Oleg's response to such demands for advice was about as direct as you can get "I'm sorry madam, I'm just a salesman. I can't tell you what your children will like. But if you want to buy something here I'll sell it to you". When he said these words - and he said them politely enough - the intending customers would inevitably become very irate and try to force him to give them advice.

Now, I'm not giving these examples as illustrations of how to cope with clients or sell toys, because clearly they are not. But they do illustrate just how much people unwittingly try to extract emotional support from others, and how let down and angry they get when they don't receive it. This is a practical problem that you will undoubtedly face when you start shooting your words from the hip.

My wife, who took over and now runs my old conveyancing practice, also showed me just how effective paying attention to this problem could be. She set out to provide the emotional support that clients obviously wanted and saw it as an essential part of her job as a conveyancer. Within a year she had increased the turnover of the practice by about a third with very little effort. For her that emotional support for the client was her being true to herself. The fact that she recognised the need in people and consciously fulfiled it was her employing one of her personal attributes. For me, I would have been hard put to offer that kind of support because I saw the job in a much more clinical, technical, legal fashion and found it very difficult to empathise with people whose world was about to come to an end because of a two week delay in a completion date. I was being true to myself also.

The message here is therefore to be fearless in communicating powerfully and truthfully your own version of the truth. If you are unwilling or unable to do even that then you will quickly fall into a downward spiral of misperception and delusion. Rather than adulterate your message you should try perhaps to be selective in where and when and how you attempt to communicate it. Casting pearls before swine is a costly and time consuming business. Yet often as teachers we must do just this, for there is no point in preaching to those who are already converted.

THE POWER OF BEING YOU

Understanding exactly who you are and how you fit into the cosmos can be a source of enormous strength. Your immediate task therefore is to see your life in terms of its overall significance, not merely how it seems when, from your limited perspective you stare out at the world and assess how it appears this particular day. Today you can be happy. Today you can be sad; you can feel successful or unsuccessful. You can view yourself in terms of the objects and circumstances that you have created around you. But none of these things is actually very important as compared with your true identity. To get an inkling about who you really are you must begin to cultivate a degree of detachment from your day to day concerns; otherwise you will be staring so fixedly at the bluebells you will overlook the vast forest in which they grow.

As a unique expression of the divine creative force learning to mould and create on the physical plane it is inappropriate for you to concern yourself with many of the promptings of your frail ego. Try putting your existence in perspective. If you knew that your next act were your last act on Earth you would be unconcerned with trivialities. You would take care to ensure that your act would be an act flowing from your heart; an act befitting and lent nobility by its expression of your infinite qualities. Try using the ever presence of your own death as an advisor to imbue your acts with strength and power so that they reflect your profound inheritance.

CHAPTER
5

MY STORY

At the age of 20 I was very nearly successful in killing myself. I took 26 Mandrax sleeping pills and several hundred Librium anti-depressants, washed down with water drunk from a dirty milk bottle. The pills only took a few moments to take effect and the cigarette that I was smoking, as I drifted off into unconsciousness, burned itself out on my left hand. I suffered a burn in my palm which shortened the ligaments of my hand and left me unable to straighten it. I was apparently dead on arrival at hospital. My head had swollen to double its usual size because of the chemical cocktail I had taken and, where I to survive, the risk was that I would become a vegetable because of the lack of oxygen to my brain. It was touch and go, but I did eventually regain consciousness after three days. After reading this book I will leave it to you to decide whether or not any significant damage was in fact done to my brain!

When at last I became fully conscious the first person I saw was a large, happy, black lady nurse; the embodiment of the Earth Mother image. She simply oozed with love and joviality. My first words to her were that she was beautiful. I was so weak I was unable to sit up, so she had me drink milk from a ceramic bowl with a spout. It was a real as well as a symbolic rebirth; coming back to life to be welcomed into the world by love and once again to be suckling milk.

The person that took that step thirty years ago is not the person that lives and breathes today, but his experiences do illuminate my work. And because of that, it is a part of my truth that personal development can begin whenever and wherever the choice is made - irrespective of one's personal background or present circumstances. I therefore speak especially to those who may have lost faith in themselves and the world in which they live. I want to shout out and tell you that strength, vitality, love and success can spring from weakness, heartache and rejection. If you have the courage and perhaps the doggedness to endure; then sooner or later you will accomplish the leap of faith necessary to assert your transcendent nature.

A child needs adequate food, shelter, clothing, water, love and stimulation. It is relatively easy for the child to recover from a temporary lack in any of these items, but if they are missing for an appreciable length of time the child's development is always stunted or blocked in some crucial way. But who that has been wounded as a child - and we all have to some degree - can precisely know where and when the child's psyche lost its elastic responsiveness to the trials of infancy. Who knows what the precise circumstances were which caused my own insecurity and emotional weakness ?

From my present perspective as a warrior the answer to this question is immaterial. But as a weak and powerless young man I would analyse my childhood circumstances ad nauseam and in my mind scatter blame where I could. As a child I was blessed with sufficient food and water but I could always point to an inadequacy of love and attention. My own mother's love was expressed through the care with which she prepared my food and the cleanliness of my clothes, but she and my father were never able to use the word 'love' to me or to express their feelings by physical contact. We all, parents included, do the best we can. But like you and I and their own forebears we can but pass on many of our own inadequacies and pain to our children.

Perhaps it was that, or perhaps it was because as a baby or very young toddler I suffered an extended stay in hospital with little human contact. It was in the days when parents did not stay with their children in hospital. I can summon up today the terror and isolation of that experience; a child screaming endlessly through the bars of a metal cot.

For whatever reasons, suffice it to say that my emotional life became stunted. It was not for many, many years before my emotional body was able to develop once more. It was many years before I was able to speak aloud that alien word 'love' It seemed to me to be a word to describe a state of affairs capable of existing only in an abstract sense, never in a concrete, realizable way.

I would remind myself how my feelings had never been acknowledged or validated as a child. I would recall the embarrassment I suffered because my parents would not buy me a pair of long trousers when all the other boys in my class wore them. And, of course, I could always point out how, despite my parents fairly comfortable means, I had very few toys; sensible things like ties and socks I naturally had in abundance.

For my early years I have mere snatches of memory. I used to practice blotting out the sections of my life that I found unpleasant to remember. As a young child we lived in Germany for a while. I remember feeling fear at the hostility expressed by German children who would throw stones at the children of the occupying powers. My only other memory there was being given, perhaps for my birthday, a small yellow car with headlights that came on when it was pushed.

I went to many different schools as the family was regularly uprooted when my father was posted from one RAF camp to another. My early school days encompassed far too many schools for me to recollect; they all seem to blur into a time of anguish for a small boy without friends being forced to eat unpleasant food which at that time in my life consisted of fatty meat and cabbage. Eventually my memories crystallise on a small village school at Stanton St Quinton, in Wiltshire. I would walk the mile or two to school and back each day along a winding country lane, which crossed over a Cotswold stone bridge, perhaps twenty feet above a stream. Sometimes, in a demonstration of bravado I would climb up this bridge from the stream bed to the bridge parapet. At school the fearsome but fair Mrs Kay singled me out as being of sufficient reliability and perhaps discretion to give me the job of purchasing her cigarettes at the local shop. She smoked Du Maurier cigarettes in an elegant red packet with silver stripes. Years later for a time I smoked Du Maurier in some homage to my memory of her. At that tender age I could run rather quickly and my breaktimes at school were devoted to running races and trying to organise vast bombing raids with seemingly hundreds of children all imagining themselves to be Douglas Bader, the legless war ace or perhaps Guy Gibson of the Dam Busters. My reading was quite good for the village school and I was given the job of helping one or two of the less able children to read. I think my time there must have been relatively happy.

I took the first part of the 11 plus exam when I was aged 9. This was apparently an intelligence test. I'm not sure what the result was but I do remember having a disastrous interview with the head teacher of Malmesbury Grammar School who persisted in asking me some mental arithmetic tests which I was unable to answer, so in retrospect I think it was almost certainly my middle class accent, clean clothes and eager demeanour that succeeded in getting me into Malmesbury Grammar School rather than my raw intelligence.

The Grammar School was then an ugly mish mash of temporary huts surrounding a lump of neo Gothic architecture. From the relative safety of a primary school that had adequately catered to my needs for several years I, a rather naive, emotionally insecure and educationally inadequate child was confronted by a very large and unsympathetic institution populated by children who all seemed to be better acquainted, cleverer and more confident than I. Life was suddenly quite unpleasant. Were it not for one poor, rather smelly and unkempt child who consistently managed to achieve worse marks than I, and whose name is still engraved in my memory, I would have been at the very bottom of the form. I was bullied and made the but of many jokes and I was very unhappy. Sometimes I would try to avoid going to school but as I could not talk about my true plight to my parents I had to rely on feigned illness, which never worked.

And yet somewhere inside me the spirit still lived and breathed and strived to shine. I walked to school every morning and passed by a small field where a horse or pony was kept. Once or twice, at the age of eleven or twelve I clambered over the railings and somehow managed to climb on the back of this animal. I had never taken any riding lessons and assumed that, given the width of a horse's back it would be a relatively easy task to stay on. The first time it was indeed relatively easy. I managed to get the horse into a bareback gallop and I measured my exploit a huge success. However, a day or two later I tried to repeat my feat but the horse walloped me with its rear hooves, knocking me over into the mud.

Once I turned on one of the boys that had teased and baited me till I could stand it no longer. I managed to overcome my fears and started a fight with him. The fight was soon stopped by the school authorities and it was decided by them that the matter would be settled in the gym with boxing gloves in place. Much to my surprise, in the ring, my opponent was no match for me. He seemed more scared than I was! By confronting my fears I had grown a little.

My academic failure at Grammar School led my parents to place me (without consultation) as a boarder in a minor public school - Sebright School at Wolverley, near Kidderminster in the County of Worcester. The school has since been taken over by the local authority because it was unable to attract sufficient pupils, despite its longish history, being founded in 1620 by William Sebright.

Even today I can feel the sinking feeling in my stomach I experienced as my father's cream coloured car drove away down the drive, leaving me for the first time outside Woodfield House, the House where I was to board. But the school proved to be a reasonably good experience for me. Flung together with a bunch of similarly placed children with tight discipline, little free time and well organised social arrangements the school became more of a home to me than home. For several years after leaving the school I would return to it as if returning to my roots. I was by the standards of the day and the customs of the school something of a tearaway, receiving in my stay 36 strokes of the cane for numerous petty offenses and being suspended for half a term for being observed drinking in a public house. I think this was something of a record.

One rather amusing incident that did manage to escape detection runs as follows: I had been teaching the Latin teacher, a Mr. Jack, how to drive. As he had not passed his driving test at that stage his elderly Daimler (complete with a fluid flywheel clutch) was parked at school. For a prank I persuaded a friend called Robin Guy to accompany me on a drive in Mr Jack's car in the middle of the night. All went well until we reached the lane outside the school. I had not put the car's lights on for fear that it would be seen, so when we drove into the country lane outside the school with its high grassy banks topped by hedgerows very little light was able to reach me and I could see practically nothing. Both my hands were on the steering wheel and I drove the car forward until I could see the silhouette of the top of the hedge against the sky and I then swung the wheel away from the bank to avoid hitting it. I shouted to Robin "Lights, Lights", meaning please put the car lights on, as I could not afford to take my eyes off the road. Just at that point the lane divided into two. Robin misunderstood my instructions and turned on his flashlight, shining it against the windscreen which reflected the light into my eyes and completely obliterated my already poor vision. The car surged blindly onwards over a ditch and into the hedge exactly at the point where the lane divided into two.

Panic struck, I ran back to the school and awoke all the other 16 and 17 year olds in my dormitory, summoning their help so they could assist in extracting the car from the ditch and the hedge. Rather to my surprise we managed to pull the car out of the ditch and most of the dormitory got a lift back to the school in the car. I spent the rest of the night pulling twigs out of the bumpers and the chassis of the car. Though I lived in fear for several weeks later the offense was never discovered nor my part in it.

I left school having scraped enough GCE 'A' levels to get me into college to study for a degree in Sociology. I had no clear idea about where my life was leading but gaining a degree seemed a good idea. I first attended West Ham College of Technology but without the strict discipline I was used to at boarding school, with no real roots and with my personal insecurities again coming to the fore I was unable to do sit peacefully by myself to do any serious study. My principle memories of that time are of spending my evenings in that well known Wapping public house The Prospect of Whitby and returning home to sleep at a time in the morning when industrious students were awakening. I think I chose to avoid taking the end of year internal examinations because I knew the results would be disastrous. Or perhaps my memory is playing tricks and I did take the end of year examinations and the results were actually disastrous. Either way, I left the college, and I decided to get a job.

After some time selling Betterwear products door to door whilst staying at my parents home in Kent I got a post seemingly more appropriate to my 'A' level status. Appointed to the Post Office in Birmingham as an Executive Officer for the first time I came face to face with what it was to really earn a living. I found myself doing a job that gave me no opportunity to use my initiative and in which every task necessitated consulting the rule book. The stark reality of life from which I had previously been shielded for the first time hit me. It was suddenly blindingly obvious that I really had to pull my finger out if I wanted to do something that would fulfil me. Whether I liked it or not, I was responsible. I became motivated for the first time in my life and, again, for the first time in my life, made a real decision, an empowering decision; a decision that was backed by commitment. I chose to do whatever was going to be necessary to complete my Sociology degree.

I wanted a fresh start, so I ignored West Ham College and instead applied to what is now Kingston University to get on to the second year of the same London University Sociology degree course. They accepted me conditionally. I was required to pass the three examination subjects that I would be examined on for the degree at the end of the second year: Statistics and Survey Methods, Economics, and Ethics and Social Philosophy. Motivationally I was a changed person. With the dread of a life sentence as a pen pusher at the Post Office hanging over me, for months I studied after work and at weekends.

Happily, I passed the three examinations without difficulty. I then spent two years at Kingston College of Technology. Emotionally, I remained a disaster area, but after two years study I did achieve a respectable honors degree. It was towards the end of my time there that I attempted to kill myself and very nearly succeeded. There were, of course, precipitating factors, but the underlying problem was my emotional weakness, my Achilles heel. Having harboured thoughts of suicide from about the age of 13 it seemed like the end of a chapter to have actually attempted it. It was at this low point, whilst still in hospital from my suicide attempt, that I made the second empowering decision of my life. I chose to take the view that life was worth living, irrespective of the pain that it had brought me and no doubt would bring to me again. Irrespective of what the future might hold for me I decided that I would never attempt to kill myself again. The psychiatrist that interviewed me as soon as I was well enough told me that people who make a serious suicide attempt will always make another attempt, and suggested that I become an in-patient for a while. I declined the offer and explained that there would be no further attempt, ever. He also seemed intrigued that, although my suicide attempt had been a serious effort, I had left no suicide note which apparently is usually the case. My reason for not leaving a note was simply that there seemed no point. Being unable to communicate effectively in life, there seemed little point in doing so from the grave. In any event, my decision to opt for life was a backstop in my subsequent emotional traumas. It put problems in their place. It determined that no problem, however large, was ever again going to produce that result. It acted to reconstruct my perceptual framework.

Years passed ; I became a salesman for an oil company, I moved jobs, I started from scratch again, I acquired skills as an accountant, and then as a property lawyer, first as a cowboy and then later as a qualified conveyancer. I learned to focus, to delegate, to manage. But my emotional life lurched from crisis to crisis and never satisfied. My first marriage broke down, my second marriage proved disastrous yet dragged on for years because of my emotional weakness; and in particular my inability to leave my children. (In the UK the mother in a divorce has to be a drug addict with several criminal convictions before custody is awarded to the father). Eventually I found the strength to leave. It became the only course of action open to me because home life had become unbearable. Ultimately my sanity was at stake, and only at that point did I leave home and stayed with a friend who lived in Birmingham.

For six months I did little but try to come to terms with my life. All I knew was that enough was truly enough. I did not ever want to repeat the same mistakes again, all of which I could see with hindsight were the product of my emotional weakness and my clouded perception. How was it possible to heal these ? My third empowering decision was to assert that there had to be a new way, a new approach, and I was not going to rest until I had found it. There was simply no other acceptable alternative. That decision began my spiritual quest.

As these events were unfolding on the emotional front, the property market hit a profound slump. I made most of my employees redundant and my own income dropped to about one third of its previous generous level. My income could not support the mortgage on the very grand marital home and the house was sold. These emotional and financial issues provided the impact that was needed to force me into beginning my spiritual search.

Though I had no answers; though I did not even know which questions to ask, I could at least see that I was overweight and needed exercise. So I decided to address at least that issue. Every night I would go for a run. I put myself on a strict diet. In about three months I lost 40 pounds and became fit. But I still remained an emotional mess. I knew that, no matter what changes might occur in my business life or in the fitness of my physical body, my emotional weakness was like an Achilles heel, an open wound, which threatened to play continued havoc with my life. There seemed to be no answer.

Access to my children was unsatisfactory. In my company they were unruly, rude and undisciplined. Their mother's contempt for me and now her outright hostility had rubbed off on them. In the absence of any supportive authority from her, access with them became unpleasant. Ultimately, and after I had gained a further measure of emotional strength I chose not to have access to them because the terms on which that access was available to me were terms on which, had I accepted them, would have involved my living a lie; the persona that would have been presented to the children would have been a persona cowed by their mother. It was not an easy decision, but it was necessary one. And once having made that decision I felt sure and comfortable that I had made the correct decision.

When one perseveres, when one has the commitment to a purpose, when there is a constant striving to achieve a goal the emotional energy and mental focus eventually begin to pay off, no matter what the circumstances. The universe hears our call and our commitment. And so it was with me. The universe brought to me the extraordinary and exceptional means to heal the emotional weakness and insecurity that had plagued me for all of my life.

I have already related in this book how a sweat lodge served to break through the very powerful emotional block which prevented me from showing any emotion, but the unconditional love that was needed to heal my emotional insecurity came from my wife Emma. How my relationship with her began is unusual.

About six months after I had left my second wife I began to do some spiritual dowsing with a pendulum. By asking numerous questions to which there can be only a 'yes' or a 'no' answer it is possible to obtain useful information from the movement of the pendulum. By such dowsing, I was given the information that I would begin a new relationship with a 23 year old female in the third week of October of that year, and

that this relationship would be permanent. The pendulum is however a
very sensitive device and can easily give false information in response to
wishful thinking. So, whilst I was naturally delighted with the news I was
nevertheless doubtful about its accuracy.

In the summer of that year, I visited my then elderly mother in Kent.
Across the road from the old people's home where she lived a hotel was
hosting a psychic / new age exhibition. I went inside and very quickly
decided to have a reading from an American whose name I think was
Ron Zubrica His psychic sense told him also that the next romantic
relationship I would have would be for life.

The evidence for romantic success seemed to be piling up, so in my
enthusiastic naivete I decided to help the process along by joining a
Spanish class. My job did not involve my meeting any single women and
I reasoned that there were bound to be some eligible females or more
precisely the 23 year old eligible female on the course. Imagine my
disappointment when September arrived, the class began and there was
no 23 year old or for that matter anyone else one who remotely
interested me.

About this time the young woman from the estate agents below my
own office happened to mention that she had a client who could see
auras, and, with my developing spiritual interest I asked her to take me
with her the next time she visited this client. An appointment was duly
made and she and I visited Sandra, her client, one lunchtime. It
transpired that she was not only a medium, but from time to time she
was also extraordinarily psychic. She told us both some interesting facts
about ourselves and then held our hands in turn. A peculiar expression
crossed her face and she reached out for both our hands again. She then
pronounced with great finality 'You Two are One'. Yes, Emma my wife
was the young woman who then worked in the estate agents below my
own office.

However, Emma, having not the slightest romantic interest in me
because of my then tyrannical, domineering and rigid attitude,
naturally denied all romantic interest in me. I on the other hand was

intrigued by Sandra's psychic pronouncement, was encouraged by the two previous predictions and interested to pursue the matter. It is not often that a 44 year old man with all the personal qualities of a bottling machine gets a look in with an attractive young woman half his age. I had been drawn to her previously, but the age gap had intimidated me and my fear of appearing foolishness had prevented me from asking her out. My relationship with her had then deteriorated to a sour grapes tyrranical attitude on my part.

Sandra then said that I would shortly encounter a blue car, that the car would have enormous impact on me and that I would buy it. That encounter with the blue car would also mark the turning point in my life. The numbers 17 and 26 were also to be very lucky for me.

What could this blue car be like? If I were to see a blue E type Jaguar I would certainly love it and want to buy it, but I would have insufficient cash. Impatient for progress, I telephoned Sandra several times to see whether a blue car I had seen was the blue car in question. She told me that I will know when I see it, there will be no uncertainty, I will love the car.

Two or three weeks later I'm driving back from Evesham on a Sunday afternoon and as I pass through Astwood Bank I see out of the corner of my eye a flash of blue at the side of the road. I'm travelling fast and I'm a hundred yards past this patch of blue. But something makes me stop and back up the car. I see this beautiful vivid blue and grey open top sports car with large faired wings looking like an old MG. It appears to be in immaculate condition, and there's a sign on it which says FOR SALE, but without any price indication. To my untutored eye the car looks to be worth seven or eight thousand pounds, which is way, way more than the cash I have available. But I decide to push the experience along a little and locate the owner, who it transpires is an engineer and who built the car from scratch. He shows me pictures of the car at Kit Car shows and I am utterly convinced that the car is wonderful. I ask the price of the car and am amazed that it is within my reach - £2,500.00. But I hold out for a bargain and offer £1,500.00. The owner says to me - "Add is made. Then I realise that I have bought the car for seventeen hundred pounds. The number 17 has already proved to be lucky. In great excitement I seek out Emma, to show her the car. I have no doubts that with the car as evidence of Sandra's psychic power she will give credence to Sandra's predictions and experiment by going out with me. She did. We began going out together in the third week of October, just as my spiritual dowsing had predicted.

Although there is a 21 year difference in our ages, although her upbringing and experience had favoured the expression of emotion and mine the opposite, although I had learned powerful focus and she had not, although she was blessed with wonderful spontaneity and I had none, although she was generosity personified but crippled by lack of reliability, whilst I was miserly and put great store by reliability, there was an undeniable unshakable bond between us. As soon as we began going out together it was as if a steel clasp had suddenly been locked into place, as though we were chained together at the hip. Our different personalities created enormous friction as our opposite natures collided. Yet the love was always there. No matter what, her love shone through. Just as a child knows that it is loved irrespective of its naughtiness, so Emma's undeniable love shone through to me. As my confidence in her love grew so did my emotional body become whole. As time passed she acquired focus and I spontaneity. She became more reliable as I became more open hearted. I began to express my emotions and she managed to exert a degree of control over hers. We both approached a middle ground away from the previous extremes of our mechanical natures. The friction, the fights disappeared. We began to harmonise. We became a powerful team.

My divorce, after several wasted years during which my now ex wife strove to unearth a non existent and undeclared pot of gold, and in which the legal profession boosted its income by over £20,000.00 in legal costs, suddenly and unexpectedly came through on the 26th of the month. How accurate you were, Sandra.

Our relationship created some surprises. Already by now accomplished as a firewalk instructor, one day I mentioned to Emma that there was a man in California who could walk on glass unharmed, and offered workshops. Her response was immediate - "You don't need to go there; you can do it". Her belief in my ability was expressed with such conviction and congruence and yet also in such a matter of fact way that I immediately accepted her belief as my own. In an instant, my beliefs about myself changed, clearing the way for the change in my personal energy and then my demonstration of this new ability.

I started collecting milk bottles and bought a thick canvas tarpaulin to lay the broken glass on. These I would carry around in the trunk of my car in readiness for the right occasion to present itself. I was accustoming myself to my newly enlarged perspective. At that time I was the healer for a psychic roadshow that toured the UK and each evening would give a demonstration of healing and personal empowerment. After a month or two I found myself in the Godiva Hotel in Coventry, and I felt the time was right. At the point where my demonstration would normally end, I laid out the canvas and the broken glass and walked across first in one direction and then the other. Absolutely perfectly. Not a scratch or even the slightest feeling of pain. It was like walking over crunchy snow.

That experience helped me to understand in a very practical way how very important and empowering is a teacher's or instructor's belief in the ability of his or her students. Emma's belief in my abilities enabled me to change my own limiting beliefs and that change in my belief created the energetic change which enabled me who weigh 15 stone, to walk unharmed over razor sharp shards of glass.

Then, after Emma and I had learned harmony and empowerment from each other came incredible joy, with the birth of our beautiful son, Jonathan, Son of Peace. Although only just over average weight at birth he was fuelled with high octane love and gained weight dramatically. As I write he is 16 months old, about 28 pounds in weight and has developed such a mighty will that it often threatens to engulf my own. I have enjoyed the privilege of being his principal carer for about a year now and although some of my plans have been temporarily put on hold my life is full of joy. His presence has completed my healing and I am now personally far better prepared to live my dreams and work my magic than before. My heart chakra, from once upon a time being like a closed bank vault door, is now fully operational.

At firewalks Jonathan is my secret weapon. As an instructor it sometimes takes a little while to shift one's focus away from the workshop participants to oneself in order to personally do the firewalk. However, this physiological shift happens instantaneously when I lift Jonathan into my arms and walk across holding him. The love just carries us over.

The extraordinary closeness of the relationship that my wife and I have has been described as that of Twin Flames; two halves of a whole identity only one of which is normally incarnated at any one time, but unusually brought together in the same incarnation to achieve some special objective. This sounds rather grand, and it would be nice to believe it. But what I can tell you is that there is an undeniable, underlying unity which locks us together. It is as if our very molecules vibrate in unison.

I hope this story serves to illustrate that it matters not where we have come from, what pain we have suffered, what injustices have been imposed on us, what inadequacies we have brought along with us. We are all wounded, some very much more than others and certainly many have suffered deeper wounds than I. But it is the task of all of us, irrespective of the extent of our suffering and pain, to transcend those limitations. By the power of our chosen beliefs and decisions we truly can discover first our own personal power and then the unity with all from which that power itself flows.

Personal Mastery and the Training of the Magus Within

CHAPTER
6

MAGICAL ACTS

The acquisition of personal power and a degree of personal mastery creates the personal qualities required of the magician; they are one and the same. By becoming able to confront your fears, by becoming able to perceive from a standpoint unaffected by fear or emotion, by imposing order and discipline on the numerous wills fighting for supremacy in your life and by forging them into a mighty singularity you create the very qualities that you need to detach yourself from the definitions that others provide for you about the workings of the world. The ability to work effective magic therefore arises as a by product of your personal transformation. It is a simple and natural technology that your new self empowers you to operate.

We are all magicians, creators of our own destiny brought about by the implacable operation of the cosmos as it goes about its business fulfiling the will of the creator and its cocreators - ourselves. Given that our individual and collective wills are generally confused, erratic and contradictory we should not be too surprised that we hardly ever seem to get what we think we want or thought we asked for.

As individuals we vary in the extent to which we have become conscious of and have refined and practiced our creative skills. Most of us create our lives in an unconscious, haphazard fashion, whilst the master creates with an unerring precision and artistry. And yet the distance between the chaotic novice and the master is small indeed. For mastery of these skills has less to do with acquiring new information and skills than with setting aside our old perceptual viewpoints; more to do with shedding limiting beliefs than in acquiring new ones. Radical change is thus merely a thought, or a few thoughts away.

As the spiritual warrior gains in personal mastery his ability to enact magic becomes infinitely greater than before, whether or not this is even realised by him. For all intentional acts are magical acts. And as we gain in personal mastery we are no longer restricted to employing the normal or usual methods of achieving our will. For example, the magician may draw back from employing direct means of achieving his goals and choose instead to adopt more indirect means. The situation is akin to that experienced by the computer programmer. First he may learn machine code; the lowest level programming language consisting of instructions expressed in binary form, capable of being interpreted by the computer as a complex sequence of ON/OFF instructions. Machine code is very time consuming and laborious to write, but it works very efficiently and underlies all other programming languages.

But, as the programmer becomes more knowledgeable he may learn higher level programming languages - languages which have words to describe complete sequences of machine code. Thus the programmer avoids the need to repeat complex coding instructions and immediately gains a vastly increased command over the computer.

The magus is like the programmer who has learned a high level programming language. He employs indirect means which although employing the same material elements (the same machine code) as do more direct and obvious interventions they do allow him a far greater degree of control. As the same elements are used there seems to the observer to be no specifically magical power at work. The results cannot (except by magical means) be explained as a consequence of the magician's operations, so they appear merely as coincidences. The power of magical operations are therefore only susceptible to statistical analysis, not individual empirical proof. So, as you become more adept your success will be demonstrated by an increasing number of fortuitous 'coincidences' or lucky breaks.

Personal Mastery and the Training of the Magus Within

CHAPTER
7

RITUAL OR CEREMONIAL MAGIC

Most magic has historically been based on ritual or ceremony, because ritual or ceremony carries with it the embedded power of those magical operators who believed in, created, sustained, followed and then ultimately drew power from the ritual they employed. To employ established ritual is therefore to lean on the creativity and the power that numerous previous generations have on the one hand created and on the other hand drawn from. It makes it easy. The only drawback in doing this is that the magic is pre-packaged; complete with the built-in limitations of its creators and perhaps certain unpleasant or at least unanticipated side-effects. You simply take it all on trust if you wish to work with it.

For ritual to be effective it must accord with our will and express it. This is obvious if we accept that ritual is primarily a tool to focus the intentions of the magician and his assistants - making them suitable vessels to channel and direct power. It is not the ritual that accomplishes the magical work; the ritual prepares us. psychologically, emotionally and spiritually. Obviously, in practice our will is intimately intertwined with ritual so it may appear that the ritual itself is the key factor, but this is not actually so.

Some ritual does, however, fulfil a secondary aim. It acts as a specific wake up call, an evocation for those thought forms and entities who are historically linked to the particular formulation of ritual employed. For example, if you wish to invoke a specific thought form or entity it may be that its characteristics or qualities require that it be addressed in a certain manner. The thought form of an Egyptian God is not going to recognise your request unless you use the same form of address as was employed in its own creation. You have no choice but to employ the appropriate Egyptian ritual.

Unless your inclination is indeed to summon up such thought forms it is no great disadvantage if you choose to avoid ceremonial or ritual magic. The cosmos provides a whole array of alternative techniques. We should remember that the source of our own magical power does not arise from the acquisition of esoteric ceremony but rather and actually more simply in our own personal mastery. If, however, you are particularly interested in ritual/ceremonial magic then I recommend you buy a book called 'The Complete Magic Primer, by David Conway which offers an excellent introduction to the subject.

It may perhaps be quicker for the average man to conduct pre-packaged ceremonial magic than for him to undertake the personal discipline and to achieve the degree of mastery needed to operate from his own magical authority, but for those who have already acquired a degree of personal mastery there need be no contest.

CHAPTER
8

PRAGMATIC & CHAOS MAGIC

Magic is the art and science of intentional action. If then we choose to dispense with ritual then we must instead rely exclusively upon the singularity and power of our own will, and to ensure that such will is in alignment or at least not out of alignment with the current of will forged by the creator. Magic that dispenses with ritual is often called pragmatic magic. However, there is often in practice an overlap between ceremonial and pragmatic magic, and some would argue that several of the procedures discussed below are strictly ceremonial. Nevertheless, I include them because I believe their prime importance lies in their ability to help focus and discipline the operator's mind.

Chaos magic represents the antithesis of ceremonial magic because it focuses on purely the personal symbolism of the operator and his access to chaos - the field of potential from which we can tap into magical forces.

SPIRIT - THE DRIVING FORCE
To the extent that we live in harmony with our spiritual essence to that extent do we become available as a conduit for unlimited power. It is only our own sense of limitation that holds us back. When we learn to

flow with the spiritual current customary limitations fall aside. Our need for sleep and recuperation reduces; our energy level increases and yet we probably eat less food.

In order to flow within this current we must learn to live in the present moment; to deal with the demands, the needs and the responsibilities only of the present moment. When we split our attention and try to focus on more than that which immediately confronts us or when we worry ourselves about what will happen tomorrow we are like a general that divides his forces; instantly his strength becomes 50% weaker and he becomes much less able to confront the immediate task. Relying on the infinite, trusting in the sustaining power of spirit involves placing your entire focus on the task that is immediately before you.

This does not mean that you should never plan, never concern yourself with what is to happen tomorrow. But what it does mean is that when you choose to plan about tomorrow's events then it is that subject that must be the exclusive object of your attention.

EMOTION - THE SWITCHGEAR

We have already discussed how the expression of emotion is a matter of choice. As the warrior grows stronger in the realisation of his or her unlimited nature the imperative quality of his emotions and other aspects of his mechancial nature subside. What once were experienced as major upsets are now experienced as mere trivialities. The warrior therefore chooses not to expend energy in the expression of needless emotion. He is to a degree detached.

This detachment is not the same as controlling the expression of our emotions. To exert a vice-like grip over our emotions suggests that we are fearful of expressing them. But it is rather that we no longer feel the need to dance to their tune. No person that is a slave to their emotions can be effective in any magical enterprise. This is not to say that they will not be successful in creating, for we all do that, but it is to say that what they create will not be a conscious deliberate and predictable consequence of their will.

"Your reason and your passion are the
rudder and the sails of your seafaring soul
If either your sails or your rudder be broken,
you can but toss and drift, or else be held at a standstill in mid-seas
For reason, ruling alone, is a force confining,
and passion unattended, is a flame that burns to its own destruction"
(The Prophet - Kahlil Gibran)

The warrior magician, then, standing alone in confident peacefulness, represents a potentiality for the expression of emotion. He is capable of choosing when, where and how to express the emotion whose potentiality lies within him. Emotion thus becomes another resource for him to employ. But this is not the pretended emotion of the actor. The emotion expressed is indeed the genuine article. The warriors choice is not to be dictated to by his emotions, by his mechanical nature. He interposes his will and chooses to employ or not to employ the emotional resource available. Thus the warrior can move from outer peacefulness to explosive emotion and back to inner calmness all in the space of 30 seconds.

The warrior becomes the magician when he or she begins to consciously employ emotion as a tool; when he consciously achieves a degree of mastery over the expression of emotion. This stage is very important. Emotional energy creates a funnel to focus and thereby control spiritual energy. Without emotion we would be directionless; full of potential but lacking any ability to realise it. Our emotions enable us to switch the direction of our focus, change our method and the degree of power employed. When we feel inspired what we experience is an intertwining of emotional and spiritual energy; a state of alignment with spirit. The warrior magician seeks to maintain this state for through it he reaches outward to mould and shape and create the world of his experience.

If our emotions are a resource, it follows that we must hone and refine them until they are a suitable channel for the containment, expression and manifestation of our will. Some types of work help us to discipline our emotions. My wife's upbringing had encouraged her to give free vent to her emotions whenever they arose. But a tiger unleashed is a tiger that controls, and sure enough, her emotions frequently controlled and exhausted her. But when she became professionally qualified and began to take over the responsibilities of my conveyancing practice, its extraordinary and contradictory demands for both accuracy and speed, were requirements that could only be met by a person whose ability, focus and knowledge were not overshadowed by emotion. Sure enough, within a very short time she developed a more detached, strategic viewpoint enabling her to conserve and manage her energy more successfully. The demands made of her were inconsistent with a high energy drain, and the growth process took over to meet the challenge. And yet all without conscious effort on her part.

SACRED SPACE

To succeed in a magical operation the magus will often consider it necessary to create or locate a sacred space or personal power spot for his work. Sacred space is not actually a precondition for successful magic but it usually makes magical accomplishment that much easier. The successful operator uses all the tools that are available to him - assuming that they are appropriate to the task in mind.

Traditionally there was little conception of creating sacred space. The art lay rather in locating it. Priests, magicians, seers or those skilled in interpreting omens would identify certain places as sacred. Such places might range in size from single trees to whole mountains. Ancient cities would often be built around the sacred space occupied by the King.

If we wish to become accomplished magicians then we need to become adept at finding sacred space or power spots - locations which help us realise our magical intent. In the workshop situation we can go as a group out of the town or city into the countryside where we are less likely to be disturbed by other people. Once there, power spots can be located by the following method: Each participants begins by spinning around quite rapidly, with closed eyes. Then, they gradually slow down at their own pace until they feel drawn to move in a particular direction. Calling out their own name again and again, they slowly feel their way forward with half closed eyes in the chosen direction. When they come to a halt they have located their personal power spot.

Once the spot has been located, its boundaries can be identified by subtle probing with your senses. If these are not distinguished by readily apparent physical boundaries the boundaries can be marked by a few stones. This is quite important because we always want to know when we are working within our power spot and when we are working outside it. When we work within it we can allow ourselves to open up

Since the magus must learn to operate in all and any conditions, with all manner of people and circumstances, no matter how seemingly inhospitable, he must be able not only to locate sacred space but to create it for himself when the need arises. This is accomplished by first defining the boundary between the sacred and the profane, the magical and the ordinary. It is best to define this boundary both spatially (e.g. within the four walls, the ceiling and floor of this room) and temporally (e.g. from 8pm to 11pm this evening). Indeed, the more precisely that the sacred space can be defined the better. Especially in difficult circumstances, it is better if the boundaries are very clearly marked and if the designated place of working is kept small. We are more able to control what happens within are small space.

The magus therefore must hold very clearly in his own mind the extent and position of the relevant boundaries. This represents part of his own clarity of purpose, expressed in his mental preparation and practical planning. The magus may also - and especially if he is working with others - create physical markings, perhaps by chalk markings, perhaps with salt, or perhaps by placing marker stones. These physical markings can be emphasised by choosing boundaries delineated by significant natural objects, or perhaps by using rugs.

Ritual or ceremonial magicians further empower this sacred space through their own time honoured rituals and create what they call a

104   Circle of Safety, the fortress which helps to protect them from the consequences of their mistakes. The creation of the magic circle by one means or another appears to be the basic requirement for all kinds of occult ceremony.

PURIFICATION

Next, the magus will cleanse or purify the area to be used. If indoors, the room will be cleaned thoroughly. He may then employ the native American technique of smudging - using the smoke from smouldering sweetgrass, sage or other herbs to purify himself and the area. The Roman Catholic Church also use this technique, swinging large smoking incense burners around the area to be used by the priest. Smudging is therefore simply immersion in sacred smoke. Instead of smudging the magus may use aromatherapy oils to good effect. The precise method employed is not important. What is important is that what is done has a precise meaning to the magus and any others that are working with him.

What the magus does by cleaning and smudging is effective because he intends it to be effective. It is in itself a magical operation. His intentions are focussed on removing all potentialities and forces which may interrupt or work against his intentions. And this clear intention is reinforced and crystallised by the physical operations undertaken to accomplish it.

It is important that these preparatory operations are undertaken without hurry and with complete dedication. In any human endeavour part of the task involves removing the obstacles, clearing the pathway before we can walk forward on it. If we omit this exercise or carry it out in a slipshod fashion we can easily stumble and fail, or, worse still, achieve objectives which we inadvertantly express but which were not actually intended. One is reminded of that irritable remark by an English King claiming divine authority "Who will rid me of this turbulent priest" which was taken by some over zealous courtier as licence to assassinate the poor cleric who had upset the king.

The size of the group that you wish to work with is a combination of personal taste and the degree to which you are able to exert firm control over the group's activities. Large groups are capable of channelling and focussing an extraordinary volume of energy through the power of their concerted will. Traditionally, the maximum number is thirteen. I personally however enjoy working with larger size groups of twenty or more but the greater the group size the greater the energy that is produced and the correspondingly greater control must be exerted to maintain the group's singularity of purpose. In a group of thirty or more it is absolutely vital to very strictly determine in advance every aspect of the work and to lay down strict operational rules.

The magus employs and directs the interactions not only between group members and himself but also between group members. As group size increases the number of potential interactions and the energy thereby created increases dramatically. Ultimately however, difficulties of control and consequent undirected unfocussed energy begin to outweigh the advantage of any increase in number of participants.

In order to forge a united will from the individual wills of the participants one must proceed slowly, ideally at the pace of the slowest participant, gently nudging the group into a steadily changing reality; a reality determined by the definitions employed by the magus, rather than the individual participants. In my work as a firewalk instructor it was some time before I began to realise that I was employing magical means to help create the empowered state required of participants to enable them to walk safely over incandescent coals. To change beliefs and perceptions the magician may employ music and dancing, sound and movement. Traditionally the magician has employed rhythmic drumming as one very effective means of creating a state of altered perception. Any and all of these tools can be used and may be effective, but whatever tools are chosen they must always be subservient to the task for which they are employed; they must not become an end in themselves.

106   Through the deployment of directed energy within the designated sacred space the space itself becomes energised, sacred. Its qualities become fixed; fixed in the mind of the magus and in the minds of any assistants/participants. Every time the space is used for the same purpose we enhance its sacred qualities and increase its power. It is therefore naturally desirable to use the same place again and again.

CHAPTER
9

MAGICAL TECHNOLOGY

This chapter describes the tools that can be used by anyone who has gained a degree of personal mastery. The procedures outlined serve to give you an immediate boost to your ability to articulate your will and to your spiritual authority.

If you think a particular operation or symbol is necessary to do the magical work then your thinking is correct. If you consider a particular ritual unnecessary, then, again, your view is correct. Today, in my view, too much is written about the need for protection and the desirability of creating a shield or cloak of protection, or light around you. To those who employ such devices they are clearly desirable. But I say that if you admit the possibility that such protection is necessary for you then so it must be. The Master's personal power, self discipline and the singularity of his will do not allow the admission of the forces or entities which are in others held at bay by the cloak of protective light.

Our sole purpose in employing symbols, visualisations, affirmations or other ritual is as tools to further refine and prepare ourselves. Symbols (which I discuss later) are there to crystallise and focus your will. If your perception were sufficiently clear and your will were strong enough you would need no such tools

PERSONAL PURIFICATION
The magus must first purify himself; make himself a fit channel for power. This is actually a natural ritual we employ whenever we have a job interview, a date or are going out to dinner with friends. We have a bath and dress in a manner suitable for the occasion. In addition to these obvious rituals the magus may take some hard physical exercise. This will burn up any stress induced chemical cocktail in his bloodstream. Three days away from alcohol will remove the last trace of it from the body. Dieting, and even abstention from sex can be employed.

The mental discipline involved in undertaking the physical purification, perhaps further enhanced by meditation, focuses our mind on the singularity of our purpose. We do not need to don weird looking clothes. The clothes we wear should however enable us to feel empowered and should demonstrate the unity of our intention. Wearing a football shirt would not, for example, demonstrate this.

These disciplines are, in a sense, merely the final icing on the purification cake. The warrior magician will already have stripped away much of his or her mental garbage and more obvious 'personality' which would otherwise obstruct the flow of his power.

PURIFY THE INSTRUMENTS
Next, any instruments that are to be used should be purified. These instruments may be as mundane as a tape recorder or as traditional as a ceremonial dagger. Our sole concern must be to determine their aptitude for the task for which they are intended to be used. Ideally, they will have been made personally by the magus, but if not, then at least they need to be purchased without haggling about the price and with concern solely for their fitness of purpose. To haggle about the price is to detract from their sacredness - their singularity of purpose.

THE MAGICAL LINK
Traditionally, it was held that any magical operation - any event that results from intentional action - involves the creation or use of a magical

link. A magical link is the medium through which our will is manifested.
Sometimes a magical link already exists, sometimes it may have to be created. We could employ magic, for example to gain the attention of the young lady in the local Blockbuster Video store with relative ease, because there are already several potential links that might be used - the most obvious being our physical presence, the shared language and the video recordings. But it would be considerably more difficult to achieve the same effect with, say, a Chinese film actress on location in Australia. We would have to overcome many purely practical difficulties to create an effective magical link.

Alistair Crowley classifies the magical link into three types:

(a) where the link involves one plane and one person - e.g. if I wish to heal my body through magical means there need be no extraneous device to make the connection between our will and the object of our focus. The link already exists

(b) where the link involves one plane and two or more persons - for example where we communicate our will through speech or some other medium to another person. The effectiveness of this link will depend entirely upon the effectiveness of the communication - upon the level of agreement as to the meaning of the symbols employed to communicate the magician's will.

(c) where the link involves two planes and two or more people - e.g. where the link has to be created in the absence of, say, a common language.

Crowley suggests that in these circumstances it requires very great magical skill to obtain satisfactory results. On the face of it magical operations of this type are very rare indeed and perhaps almost impossible to achieve. But in Doug Boyd's book 'Rolling Thunder' the medicine man Rolling Thunder of the Shoshone tribe was able to induce a heavy downpour of rain out of season. Likewise, in the 1950's Dr Rolf Alexander gave a number of demonstrations of his ability to make clouds disappear before numerous observers. Photographs showing a 1954 demonstration appear in his book 'The Power of the Mind'.

My own view is that we must start from the premise that all events and entities are but different aspects of the whole and, as such, there is an underlying magical link already forged between them. It is the strength of our will that we must use to cross the seeming void.

PERSEVERANCE

As a young sociology student in the late sixties I attended a middle of the road London college. There was a fellow student who was deeply committed to a very left wing viewpoint. By the sheer power of his commitment and personal congruence he managed to shift the political centre of gravity of the college dramatically to the left practically single-handed. His message was some radical revolutionary brand of socialism that very few students actually embraced, but such was the enthusiasm and strength of this young man's vision that the persistent repetition of his deeply held beliefs lent them a credence and a respectability previously lacking. He managed to achieve an enormous change in the political perceptions of the students.

The message here is that if you are deeply committed, if you inflame your will to an extraordinary pitch, if you communicate your will congruently your ability to influence events is strong indeed. The power and consistency of your will must sooner or later pay off. It is as if you must first overcome the intrinsic inertia of the universe. In the absence of an obvious magical link this at first sight appears to be an awesome task, yet by holding fast to our vision we do succeed. Events do begin to work out as we want them. Soon what was inertia becomes impetus or kinetic energy and then the very bulk of the universe comes to work for us. We ultimately set in motion a chain of events that become difficult if not impossible to prevent.

THE EGREGORE

There is a concept in magic called the egregore, which means the community of ideas, symbols, emotions that a particular group of people have, over time, built up. Thus each religious faith, each magical group, each country will have its own egregore. To the extent that we can identify the egregore of a particular group to that extent we can employ it as a magical link. Likewise, if we employ the egregore that is appropriate to our circumstances and attainments then we can draw power from that connection. If, however, we attempt to link into an egregore that is inappropriate - for example by attempting to utilise in a Western context Hindu traditions we are likely to be unsuccessful.

Much has been written about the native American egregore or tradition and several books have extolled the virtues of employing that tradition in the UK. But the fact is that the native American egregore does not as yet have very strong roots in the UK and if you try to employ its magical concepts within the UK you may well create confusion and little else. If you wish to experiment with native American shamanism I suggest you purchase an airplane ticket. You are likely to be more successful if you involve yourself with Celtic traditions.

THE MAGICAL OATH

The Magical Oath is the verbalisation of and commitment to a particular purpose. It is the fullest expression of the magus' will and it binds him for ever. The Oath is usually associated with ritual magic but its use is nevertheless a useful discipline because it serves to unravel the contents of the magus' will and clarifies his objectives. And if he is to be utterly and irrevocably committed it would be well for him to articulate precisely his intent, lest his success brings with it some unfortunate and unintended consequences.

In ritual magic the oath is usually sworn as follows: The magician stands in the centre of the circle and strikes a bell to alert the attention of his assistants and the cosmos. He then declares who he is, his status in the magical tradition and a description of the events that have led to the present position. He then states the purpose of the ceremony and why the ceremony and its success is necessary. He then calls upon God or other powerful entity to witness his Oath. Then the magician swears solemnly that he will perform his oath, that nothing shall prevent him from performing it, that he will not leave the required magical operation until it has been successful. He strikes the bell again.

Although I have never myself sworn a magical oath in this formalised way, the decision I made when embarking on my spiritual quest (described in Chapter 5) operated in a very similar way. The magical oath represents a daunting level of commitment; a level of commitment only really capable of being appreciated by those who have already understood exactly what commitment is all about.

A century ago members of the order of the Golden Dawn magical order were required to swear an oath committing themselves to the 'Great Work':- "I further promise and swear that with the Divine Permission I will from this day forward apply myself to the Great Work - which is to purify and exalt my Spiritual Nature so that with the Divine Aid I may at length attain to be more than human, and thus gradually raise and unite myself to my Higher and Divine Genius, and that in this event I will not abuse the great power entrusted to me"

The Oath therefore acts as a very formal and, if you like, ritual demonstration and affirmation of your will. It serves to create a commitment that is not merely personal, but one that is announced to the cosmos.

AFFIRMATIONS

Correctly formed affirmations work because they are spiritual commands. We do not say "I wish to be healthy" or "I wish to be free", we say instead "I am healthy", "I am free". Expressed in this way affirmations are commands to the universe.

Affirmations employed by the average person often fail to work. Why is this? The answer is simple. The average person is a mass of contradictions, with no singularity of will. Repeating an affirmation ad nauseam merely announces these contradictions to the cosmos. When an affirmation is issued correctly - with clear intention, a singularity of will and backed by the strength of our focussed emotion - it need be issued once only. As such it represents an absolute expression of our will.

Repetition of our affirmation serves only a useful purpose if we are training ourselves to get it right. To repeat an affirmation mindlessly is merely wasting everyone's time. Our attention should therefore be on getting our commands right the first time.

When affirmations are used correctly they can have a powerful, immediate effect. I quite often use them in my firewalk workshops. It is interesting to note that it is always the one or two people in a firewalk workshop who have difficulty in expressing an acceptable affirmation that also have difficulty in actually doing the firewalk itself.

PRAYER

Prayer is a form of magical act because, in prayer, we are intending to produce a particular result. It is an expression of our will. Those who pray are probably aghast at this suggestion. But can we really believe that there is an all powerful entity that sits in judgement of us as we pray, determining which prayers are worthy of being answered and which are not; determining who amongst us deserves to have their prayers answered, and who do not? I think not.

Often prayer does not work. Why ? There may be several reasons for this - for example, the prayer may be expressed in a meaningless litany or it may have been undertaken in a state other than the correct state of spiritual consciousness. If we pray for the life of a friend or partner from the standpoint that death is the big termination rather than the sloughing off of the material body, then clearly our prayers will be riddled with our own fears and limitations. If we pray to an all powerful entity then we deny our own spiritual power.

In other words, we are not coming from the right place; from the place which knows the underlying unity of all and from which we may assert our spiritual authority. Prayer is in fact a fundamentally flawed magical technique simply because it denies this unity and also disempowers the person praying by denying his or her spiritual authority. It is therefore a tribute to the beneficent working of the cosmos that prayer works at all, given the garbled and confusing communication that prayer usually is.

When prayer works it works primarily because it serves to communicate, however inadequately, our will. The more fervently we pray and the more of us that pray together the greater do we express the singularity and power of our collective will enhanced by our emotional force and the greater probability therefore that our prayers will produce a desirable result. Prayers are therefore not answered or left unanswered any more than we can say that the video recorder is unhappy with us if an electronic glitch stops it from working properly.

COMMANDS

All spiritual commands need to be undertaken in the awareness of your spiritual capacity. This is essential because it is this which establishes your authority to decree.

If you are in two minds about something, the result is confusion - spirit is unable to obey contradictory instructions. To decree successfully you must first see not only yourself but also the subjects of your intended decree in their spiritual capacity. In this way you will see and address not their apparent weakness, not their evident inadequacy, but rather their divine spiritual qualities.

At this point your will is employed to blast your decree into the cosmos. Once your decree has been issued spirit takes over the task and performs the actual work. In magical operations we may try to help spirit do its job by, in advance of our decree, creating or firming up one or more magical links, but once the decree is issued we leave well alone.

If we get impatient with apparent inaction or if we are uncertain about whether we will achieve the desired result and then try to once again reaffirm our will by further decree then we may bring the whole under-lying process that we have set in motion to a halt. To repeat our actions is to express our lack of confidence in our earlier operation and to recall the power which originally issued our decree. Therefore all good books about affirmations and prayer will tell you that you should adopt the belief that your affirmation, prayer or decree has already worked.

You should remember that the pace of the cosmos appears to be a lot slower than is often suggested by our predisposition toward impatience. Time is not merely a quality needed to demonstrate that our thoughts and intentions precede the physical manifestation of events. Time also provides a space to create the required changes and growth in you, the dictator. Frequently I have felt frustrated by seemingly unwarranted delay only to find that when I the person reached the appropriate stage in my personal development the cosmos promptly provided the decreed result with immaculate timing. The cosmos knows better than we do.

Issuing spiritual commands is not that difficult once we have acquired a degree of personal mastery. The problems and apparent no-shows arise from two main sources : (i) because we don't want what we think we want - our energy flits about from one objective to another (ii) we lack confidence in our abilities and through impatience try to tinker with a perfectly good command.

A pre-requisite for the fulfilment of your commands is that they should not only be in your best interest but also be in the best interests of others. That your commands should be in the best interests of others flows from your position as part of the cosmic One. To strike out against another is to strike out against yourself. Therefore it is wise when framing your decrees to include the proviso that no harm shall come to others.

THE CREATIVE POWER OF THOUGHT

Nearly everything you see has to some extent been modified created or controlled by the human mind. And before that fashioning, control or creation could take place the thought form of the finished product was constructed in the human mind. Thought is creative, constructive; the mould for energy. and the interface between the material and non material planes.

Every thought represents a physical potentiality. We are today the result of our past thinking. Tomorrow we shall be the result of what we think today. We create our own personality by the selectivity of our thoughts - by the thoughts which sometimes energise, promote and encourage, and sometimes by the thoughts which discourage and disempower.

We develop our power to consciously create our circumstances - our magical mental power - by constantly exercising our mind, by consciously focussing and giving energy to those thoughts that are positive and productive. The more we exercise our mind in this way the more do we become able to precisely articulate the creation of what we desire. This process includes employing one's imagination to visualise the desired outcome. But those who, like myself, find visualisation diffi-cult, should not despair. It is sufficient to think about the desired out-come in detail.

Why is it that some people seem to attract wealth, power and success with little apparent effort and others achieve success only with great struggle and much work ? Why is it that some never achieve success? The answer lies in the functioning of our mind. It has purely to do with the ability of some people to organise, discipline and control the creative power of their thoughts. Unless these qualities are developed our creative powers are squandered. The creative power of thought is a power given to all, irrespective of our wealth, status or intelligence. If we are in a mess now then it is a mess that we ourselves have created by not learning and practising how to use the skill. It takes time and effort to learn how to read and write; we are given the ability, but the effort must be made. The same applies with our creative abilities.

Since it is our thoughts that create, it follows that the clearer our thoughts, the more complete is our mental patterning of what we desire. Further, the greater the intensity of our passion the greater is the impetus given to our thought. To create the mental blueprint that the cosmos needs to work with, we need to be very clear about what it is that we want; we need to visualise or think in great detail how all the parts hang together. If some of the parts conflict we may achieve nothing or we may find ourselves trapped in a nightmare of unintended consequences. We may even find ourselves swinging from one extreme

Also, we should ensure that the vision we create does not hold within itself some aspect of our present limitations. If we are fearful now, do not imagine a future where that fear still subsists. Sweep all limitations aside in the grandeur of your vision. When our vision is complete, when we are excited by its impending arrival, when our will and focus are irrevocably committed then we release our vision to the cosmos in the certain knowledge that the cosmos is right now putting the building blocks in place.

This does not mean that we have to sit back and do nothing until our vision suddenly appears in the physical plane. Manifestations on the physical plane are created out of the physical plane. I am reminded of the story where the fervently religious man, trapped on the roof of a house surrounded by rising flood water repeatedly turned away offers of help from passing boats etc. sure in the knowledge that the Lord would come to his aid. Eventually the man drowned. God was rather exasperated and pointed out to the man that he had been more than a little stupid. God had sent him two rowing boats, a power launch and a helicopter to save him. In what possible way did the man imagine God was going to save him?

Our practical responsibility is simply to pick up and use the tools that the cosmos supplies. Provided we hold firm to our vision we shall not go too far astray and such apparent detours as befall us will almost certainly be necessary to prepare us personally for the vision we have created.

There is however one trap we must avoid. Whilst it is certainly imperative to create a clear and complete vision, what we must not do is to construct a vision of the precise means that will take us from where we are now to where we wish to arrive. To do so would be to pre-empt the power of spirit to do its job. Likewise, if you try to second guess spirit or accelerate the process by constructing steps in advance you are simply wasting energy and may possibly be obstructing spirit. You must have patience. Our responsibility is to form the finest creative projectile, to fire it off with the greatest emotional charge we can muster and then to rest easy in the firm expectation the cosmos will bring about what we desire.

SIGIL MAGIC

Sigil magic is another method of refining and crystallising our will. This method falls within the category known as 'Chaos Magic'. The system developed by Austin Osman Spare is perhaps the best known and also the simplest. Sigils are prepared by converting the letters forming the sentence of our declaration of intent into a symbol. Any letters which are repeated in this sentence are omitted and the letters remaining are then fused into a symbol with certain strokes (at your discretion) emphasised or increased in length and others reduced in length or otherwise stylised. The book "Practical Sigil Magic" by Frater U D published by Llewellyn is an excellent primer on the subject. Similarly, sigils can be prepared by drawing symbolic or pictorial representations of events which can then be stylised further into the sigil proper. Indeed, a sigil can be created by any means convenient to you. What is however of vital importance is that the sigil must be created by you and not someone else. The sigil you have prepared can then be activated or 'charged' by impacting your emotion and will upon them.

CHAPTER
10

LIVING IN ABUNDANCE

WE ARE ALL GIFTED CREATORS

Wealth can be obtained in numerous ways, but many of us find its acquisition extremely difficult. Even when we are successful there are very often unpleasant side-effects that we had not anticipated. For though we are all magicians, gifted creators of our experience there is a wide gulf between the unconscious, unfocussed and haphazard process of creation practiced by the vast majority of us and the conscious creative process undertaken by the master, whose abilities have been honed and focussed to create with precision the required result and no other.

This haphazard quality is but a reflection of ourselves - our confusion between conflicting desires, priorities and a fear produced lack of congruence between our thought, words and deeds. But the Master, whose personal qualities reveal a clear channel for the expression of the singularity of his will and a near perfect congruence, creates a precise and orderly reflection of his vision. The spiritual way to wealth therefore demands personal congruence. There are no short cuts.

PROSPERITY CONSCIOUSNESS

For the reasons given above many of those who seek wealth and who attend prosperity workshops are destined not to get it or to lose it once they have stumbled across it. The Bible says "seek ye first the kingdom of God and all these things will be added unto you". In other words wealth and prosperity are by-products of spiritual progress - the natural products which flow from a certain type of consciousness - which I call 'Prosperity Consciousness'. This consciousness can arise only after certain fundamental personal issues have been confronted and to some degree mastered. Hence there is doubtful merit in offering a prosperity workshop to the general public. To be successful such a workshop requires a much more select group.

What then is Prosperity Consciousness ? Briefly put, it is an awareness of and a reliance on the knowledge that the cosmos is a vast repository containing all that we will ever need, combined with a certain deftness in accessing that abundance. That deftness involves learning how to operate a relatively simple piece of technology - the spiritual fork lift truck which whizzes around the storehouse collecting goods to order. And as with all skills involving dexterity it takes just a little time and practice. We must first acquire a certain basic level of spiritual coordination (personal mastery) before we can handle the intricacies of rear wheel steering and operating the lift mechanism on our truck

MONEY AND STABILITY

Acting out our daily lives in the sure knowledge that the cosmos provides for our every need lends a sureness and confidence inspiring quality to our actions. Just as banks and other financial institutions receive money from us as deposits because of our confidence in their financial probity, wisdom and stability, so the natural stability and confidence we radiate when we have wealth serves to attract more of it. We can state a Law here: Money is drawn to Stability and Confidence. Differently formulated we may say that money runs away from fear and instability. Thus, if we don't actually have much money our first task is to create for ourselves the feeling of abundance and the resulting stability and confidence needed to attract it or at least not to have it run away

Since your thoughts are always creative, the act of asking in prayer for anything - money included - is an expression, an affirmation of your limited perception that you have a desire for an unfulfilled need. It is an instruction to the cosmos that the something that you ask for is not to be there for you. It is also a prayer which contradicts the Law of Supply (See Chapter 13). The correct prayer is therefore never a supplication, but rather a belief, an expression of gratitude for our present abundance.

Some people find this point very difficult to grasp, so I will pursue the point further. Let us take an example. If we strongly affirm from the heart that we are powerful, as we do sometimes in the firewalk workshop, then that affirmation serves to empower us. The universe hears the affirmation and confirms it by saying 'yes, that is exactly what you are, powerful'. If, on the other hand, we affirm from our heart that we want to be powerful, the universe hears us and confirms right back 'yes, that is exactly what you are, wanting to be powerful'. Do you get the point? So its no use affirming that you want to be wealthy; for the universe will merely confirm your present state of wantingness. Instead, we must powerfully affirm "I am so happy, so blessed, so grateful to be wealthy". And the universe then responds by manifesting the truth which you assert.

The means of communicating our desires is therefore well established and waiting to be used. But the purity, clarity and congruence of the prayer we create cannot be other than a reflection of ourselves. To be a successful magician you must pursue your mastery with vigour.

ARE YOU WORTHY TO RECEIVE ?
Do you truly feel worthy to receive ? If our beliefs, our thoughts betray our feelings of unworthiness we despatch to the cosmos a message that we do not in fact wish to receive our full measure of abundance. It was not until I experienced confusion and reluctance over accepting from my wife a beautiful chocolate rabbit at Easter did I realise that the child in me felt unworthy to receive such an expression of love. This started

me thinking about some of my other idiosyncrasies. I wondered at the lengths I would go to and the smug satisfaction I expressed when I succeeded in obtaining a 'bargain'. After a lot of thought I came to the conclusion that my feelings of worthiness were indeed limited. If the article cost too much or was a too frivolous expression of love then I judged myself unworthy to receive. And, of course, if you truly do obtain a 'bargain' the suggestion is that the seller has not been quite as astute as you, the purchaser. This all implies a zero-sum game where for someone to gain another has to lose - a very limiting vision of the cosmos which also contradicts the Law of Supply

If we do not feel sufficiently worthy we put a low figure on the value of the product or service that we provide. Again, our low price asserts a limiting vision of the cosmos where only those who wish to spend a small sum of money will be attracted by what we have to offer. So we become busy fools, selling our product or service at a price too low to create the time or money needed to enjoy the fruits of our labours.

OUR CONNECTION WITH THE COSMOS

Self-worth is an expression of our connection with the cosmos. When we truly feel and acknowledge our unique expression of divinity; our personal expression of the One God, our magical power reaches its zenith. Self worth is unconnected with the role we play in life, the size of car we drive or the value of the house we own. We can contrast self-worth with self-importance, which is most assuredly connected to our status in life and the material possessions we surround ourselves with, and which serves to separate us from the divine Oneness.

As we open our hearts to our part in the divine Oneness, our relationships lose their judgemental quality, our life takes on a strategic quality and our limited conception of money changes. Our feelings about money change and we open up to its flow just as we open up to the other flows of energy within the divine Oneness. No longer is it necessary for us to scoop out pocketfuls of the stuff. Suddenly we are in the midst of a broad river of energy which can become anything we want it to be.

As we lose self-importance and gain self-worth our need to distinguish ourselves from others by the material symbols of wealth and accomplishment falls away. They are no longer needed to support our need for self-importance. This does not mean that we necessarily make do with second hand clothes and live in a caravan. What it means is that we are no longer driven to have desires for certain material possessions. We have acquired a degree of detachment.

So, as we refine our consciousness and open our hearts to our divine connection we become increasingly able to create with precision the objects of our desire, yet our desires become less demanding; we no longer need impressive material circumstances. Our material circumstances are more likely to reflect our needs as dictated by our inspiration. Wealth and abundance is therefore not merely the accumulation of cash, it is a balance between our desires and our ability to satisfy those desires.

On the one hand wealth can provide a degree of personal freedom, but on the other hand the maintenance of substantial wealth tends to involve a degree of responsibility and commitment which may limit a person's freedom. And yet, if we manifest money without any responsibility - for example, by winning the lottery, we lose the spice that makes the game worth playing. True mastery of abundance in practice therefore involves work that is financially rewarding, stimulating, challenging and enjoyable .

Personal Mastery and the Training of the Magus Within

CHAPTER
11

SACRED OBJECTS, SYMBOLS & TALISMANS

SACRED OBJECTS

Sacred objects are objects imbued with power. They are objects which, like sacred space, can be discovered or created. Any object that has been the subject of an act of will becomes a talisman. Repeated acts of will impress on the talisman its fitness for the purpose of that act.

Sacred objects or talismans store power and enable it to be passed from person to person, from place to place and from time to time. They act like a battery - storing up energy until it is needed to be used. They may also be used as channels or transmitters, enabling energy to be moved from place to place.

We give objects power in a variety of ways. We may consciously focus our energy on the object, perhaps charging up a crystal. A word written on a piece of paper as an affirmation can be an object of power. Anything that we regard as lucky will take on the qualities of a sacred object. Ultimately, following the principle that energy follows thought, anything that we intend giving our power to receives it.

Creating sacred objects can however be counter-productive. Since they are often small and transportable they can be lost or stolen. When this happens their owner very often feels anxious and disempowered.

126   Sacred space on the other hand cannot be lost or stolen, but it can be defiled. The magus is therefore wary about discussing his sacred objects or revealing them. He will often carry them around with him, sometimes in what is often called a medicine pouch around his neck. Merely by being with him they are constantly being recharged.

SYMBOLS

Safer in many ways to employ are symbols. Symbols are conceptual objects - objects which therefore cannot be lost or stolen. They also have the added advantage that, once learned, they are easy to carry around inside one's mind and are readily available for use when needed.

Those who use Reiki - the art of channelling universal life energy - are taught at the second degree stage three symbols which are employed to activate and manipulate the energy. Those taking the third or masters degree learn a fourth symbol which empower them to carry out the attunements (or initiations) which are given to students. These symbols are extraordinarily effective. Reiki, whether realised by its practitioners or not, is actually a profound demonstration of magic at work.

The effectiveness of a symbol depends in part on its design, in part on the extent to which it is 'charged' by its creator, and in part on the extent to which it becomes an integral part of a magical lineage or egregore. The Reiki symbols maintain and are enhanced in their power by their repeated acceptance and use by generation after generation of initiates.

In a broader context, and especially in advertising and public relations work we encounter logos which, by their eye catching, unique design and appropriateness symbolise the type of work undertaken by the company or the particular impression that is sought to be conveyed by the company about itself. The logo becomes a crucial part of the image building process and multinational companies and international enterprises in particular often spend hundreds of thousands of dollars attempting to create and maintain a suitable image. You may consider such money wasted, but consider for one moment how much work a company would get if its logo were a swastika. This gives you some idea of just how important it is to get symbols right.

The recognition of some symbols is very widespread. The crucifix in predominantly Christian countries carries with it a bundle of meanings. Likewise, the bible itself symbolises a certain collection of beliefs. Even those who do not accept the bible as literally true are subconsciously aware of its power as a symbol. I once did some pendulum dowsing over a variety of books, including the bible. The only book that caused a response was the bible; there was no response over the other books because they symbolised nothing; they held no power. I would like to try the same experiment with a copy of Hitler's Mein Kampf; my guess is the pendulum would react violently, but perhaps in the opposite direction.

Noam Chomsky has argued that the underlying rules of grammar are similar, irrespective of the particular language. If this is so then it must follow that to some significant degree the structure of language is biologically determined and transmitted through our genes. In other words, our ability to communicate is possible because the framework of rules needed to establish any form of communication is already hard wired into us. That so, it is likely that some symbols are more likely to resonate with that hard wiring than others; certain symbols must be more effective than others irrespective of the culture or the country concerned. I will leave it to you to discover what those symbols might be!

Symbols can lose their power if they are exposed to profanity. For their power to remain intact they must be recharged and treated with respect by those who use them. To ensure that symbols are not treated irreverently they are often hidden by a veil of secrecy. For many years the Reiki symbols were kept strictly secret. The fact that they have been published now for several years will, I suspect, reduce their effectiveness as they become increasingly exposed to the profane gaze of unbelievers.

The magician can develop any system of symbols he chooses; the key is to ensure that he is perfectly clear about the meaning he attributes to each symbol. Just as it is immaterial the actual meaning that a tarot reader gives to a card provided he or she always assigns that same meaning to the card, so it is immaterial the meaning we initially assign to each symbol we wish to use provided that our meaning is clear and unambiguous and is always employed consistently. It is only when, due to our inexperience, our lack of confidence or our sheer laziness we may get confused or make mistakes and thereby create unintended consequences. In the words of an advertisement I read in the English "Prediction" magazine - 'magic requires utmost precision practice'. And so it does.

Whatever system of symbols we employ they will gain in power directly according to the extent to which we work with them and employ them. To begin with our symbols might be rather dull and lifeless - mere intellectual expressions (though the practitioner actually ought really to create a symbolism which inspires him). But with continued use the symbols will take on a life, a power of their own. They will store the power that you introduce to them and then later you will find that they begin to feed that power back to you. This is exactly what happens when you learn how to read the tarot. You purchase a tarot pack which you like the look of. Then you learn learn the meanings for each card and the pack begins to have an energy of its own. That energy is energy that you have introduced to the pack and which enables you to read the tarot.

TALISMANS
The word talisman derives from the Greek TELESMA meaning consecrated object. It is an object which often, through ceremony, or perhaps merely by its creators focussed intent has become energised. Sometimes distinguished from the talisman is the amulet, which tends to be regarded as an object which protects its owner from unfavourable influences. To create a talisman there are a number of points to consider:

Purity - The material to construct a talisman should ideally be new, so that it contains no previous influences. If the material to be used is not new then you should clean and purify it with soap and water and then rinse with cold water. If the material to be used is metal then you can also plunge it into fire. Sometimes a banishing ritual is employed. Circle the object three times saying over it "In the name of the Powers of Light, Life and Love may all evil and hostile influences depart hence - NOW" If the ritual knife or athame is employed the magician should visualise a ray of light issuing from its point to the object, dissolving and removing anything undesirable.

In certain circumstances you might want to create a talisman that you do not want to purify because of its already benign influence - perhaps because it is imbued with power from a ritual or tradition that you wish to use. But be wary of unwanted unforeseen or undesirable influences. If you are in possession of an object which, whilst not a talisman as such, is likely to be causing adverse influences then you can do no harm by purifying it.

Permanency - Some materials are fragile and likely to be impermanent, such as paper. But if the symbolism is complex and the time available minimal it may be that paper is the only realistic medium. If there is more time available you can create ceramic or metallic talismans. You may even choose to construct the talisman by reference to the traditional magical correspondences. A talisman designed to arouse and invoke the force of Venus (traditionally the ruling power of nature and love) would therefore be fashioned from copper.

Charging the Talisman - The power and intensity of your will is what gives your talisman its power. Properly charged, the talisman is able to do what you cannot do. You are unable to maintain your emotions at fever pitch all the time. Yet captured in the talisman is that power held in suspension, undiluted by the subsequent slackening of your emotional pitch.

To charge the talisman hold it in your hands concentrating with supreme intensity on the quality you wish to instill in the talisman. Visualise an enormously powerful charge building up in yourself. Let you emotions become aroused. Eventually, when your emotions are inflamed to a fever pitch you release the energy into the talisman, visualising the charge pouring through your body and arms into the talisman.

Locking into an Egregore - By locking into an egregore we extract from it the power provided by its history, its community of ideas and tradition - a collection of thought forms and symbolic references which serve to empower the talisman. When we buy a crucifix and wear it around our neck we are locking into the Christian egregore.

Purchasing a Talisman - Unless you want to use a talisman purely as a piece of decoration or jewellery it is vital that you design, construct and energise your own. By investing your own energy in that process you are making the talisman your own. It becomes an extension of your will in the very process of its creation and your efforts lend it power.

THE PENTAGRAM OR PENTACLE

The Pentagram or five pointed star is a traditional magical symbol which goes back to Pythagoras and beyond. His followers used it as a badge. To the magician, it symbolises the four elements of the material world being ruled over by the power of the mind, the topmost point of the star. Reversed, with the point downward, the pentagram symbolises spirit hidden in matter. Satanists also see in the inverted pentagram the face of the goat god, with the two uppermost points representing its horns.

The pentagram is drawn with one continuous line and is often enclosed within a circle, representing infinity and eternity.

THE WAND

The wand is a symbol of authority. It exists today in various guises - the sceptre of the monarch, the swagger stick of the army officer and, of course, the ceremonial wand of the magician, who uses it as an agent of transformation and to direct power.

Traditionally, the wand was fashioned from hazel wood cut from the tree at sunrise. Today, wands can be enhanced by the addition of one or more crystals. Very fine wands can be purchased, but they will not be as effective as a wand that you create yourself. Your wand should be energised in the same way as a talisman.

CHAPTER
12

THE MAGUS

THE AUTHORITY OF THE MAGUS

Acting in consciousness of your physical existence you are accustomed to issuing orders which result in physical consequences. You give instructions to your body and your body responds. The underlying spiritual connection between your will and its expression in the physical plane is irrelevant to you.

When you act in consciousness of your mental existence you give instructions to your mind and your mind produces non-physical expressions of your will. Again, the underlying spiritual connection between your will and its expression in the mental plane is irrelevant to you.

Now, if we act in spiritual awareness - in awareness of our existence as spiritual beings - we are able to direct events on the spiritual plane. Our authority to do this rests upon our each carrying within us the divine spark. This authority is vested in us irrespective of our physical, mental or spiritual development. It resides within because it is a function of our divine potential, not our day to day limitations we experience within the physical plane.

Our divine authority means that our will, our wishes should be

132 expressed as commands, not as prayers; as instructions, not requests. When we pray, we give away our power. When we assert or command we retain our power and our word goes out with the power of divine authority behind it. However, whilst we may have divine authority, we don't always have divine understanding and things therefore often don't work out as we wish. Unless our instructions are capable of activating and operating within divine law (the rules of the game in which we all participate) then no amount of this misdirected effort is going to produce what we want.

There are many reasons why we may fail to achieve what we desire, some of which I have mentioned previously. We may fail to frame our intentions with sufficient precision; we may fail to commit ourselves completely; our desires may be mutually exclusive, for example. If what we want runs counter to divine law we may get not what we want but perhaps some unexpected result.

And, though we may all have divine authority it is also true that those with little spiritual understanding and development will inevitably find it more difficult to produce results with precision.

PURIFICATION

Our development as spiritual beings is largely a matter of personal purification; of recapturing our essence. It involves throwing out much of the mental garbage which passes as our personality and becoming as free as we may be of any sense of limitation, prejudices and predispositions, of faulty imperitives and fears. Our perceptions and thoughts need to be released from error. To become a successful magician it is not necessary that you reach the summit of spiritual growth. What is necessary is that your will has at the very least overcome fear as a directing force and that you have become resistant to intimidation. These criteria are simple to state but in practice for many people quite difficult to achieve, but they are the hallmark of the true warrior-magician.

All of us live in a complex social world full of interrelationships, full of emotional, physical, financial, legal, practical and other types of considerations, hooks and snares. To be truly free as a directing force and to become incapable of intimidation it is probably necessary for some of us to ruthlessly prune our lives until they are organised in a tight bundle over which we are fearlessly able to employ our will. This process may take years to accomplish and may be accompanied by some pain and heartache as our warrior will expands.

The magician must always strive to remain the warrior - in, but not of the world. He is able to direct its flow, but the world does not direct his flow. Eliphas Levi said "the Magus thinks and wills; he loves nothing with desire; he rejects nothing in passion". His drive is toward perfecting himself. And this, if you recall is the worthy object of the true magus pursuing the Great Work..

By accepting this goal - perhaps under your own magical oath - you will program yourself to eliminate the imperitives which now cause you to function mechanically and to develop your essence and your ability to align with spirit. By making an Oath that your supreme objective is to perceive clearly and to think and choose with clarity and wisdom, and by instructing your subconscious mind to eliminate any error thoughts and feelings, you set in motion an internal chain of events capable of transforming your experiences and their hold over you, and of releasing you from the constraints of the past. You thereby pass ultimate authority to your Higher Self. If you choose to make such an Oath it is wise to include in it your specific authority for your Higher Self to take over the decision making process in instances where your perception and conscious thought processes are faulty. An example follows:-

"O Great Spirit of which part resides within me I promise that from this moment my mind my body my will shall be directed to the purification of my thoughts and perceptions, and to the elimination of error thoughts

I irrevocably authorise my Higher Self to overrule and neutralise such of my decisions that derive from any such erroneous perceptions and thoughts that I may have in the future and to substitute for those

134   decisions other, wiser decisions so as to bring my consciousness and my will into alignment with Spirit"

The capacity to successfully demonstrate our magical abilities lies in all of us. The tragedy is that most of us never go beyond the very preliminary stages of the art. Our power is potentially infinite, yet most of us never recognise this and fewer still learn to employ it in their lives.

SACRIFICE

The path toward achieving and demonstrating our power opens up fairly readily once we are committed to finding it. Commitment is therefore a prerequisite; commitment in the strong sense that is employed elsewhere in this book; the commitment that admits no excuses and where the body, the mind and the spirit if necessary are all pledged as resources to achieve a stated goal. This degree of commitment necessarily involves sacrifice.

This sacrifice is the 'little death' often associated with initiatory rituals. By pledging our lives we are reaching out and going beyond them; affirming that our existence cannot be reduced to our physical bodies. When we do this we are facing our fears squarely and completely; we look death in the eye and choose to ignore the screams of the ego's attachment to the physical body. We take a giant leap forward.

Be aware that, if you wish to access your highest potential; if you wish to grasp the infinite, you may need to sacrifice many of those things that your ego holds dear; many of those things which enable you to feel puffed up with pride but in reality merely act as a barrier and shield between your real identity and those that surround you. Your house is not you; your cars are not you; your spouse is not you; your children are not you, your possessions are not you. There is nothing wrong with any of these things but your attachment to them is your attachment to the physical plane. And be wary unless they also operate to support your ego.

Where is your centre? Are you able to find the core that stands alone when the quirks of your personality have been discarded? The less baggage you carry the faster your journey will be. The measure of your progress does not lie in the accumulation of skills but rather in the degree to which you have discarded the obstacles which cast shade on your perception and darken the light from your heart.

The true magus has plumbed the depths of his soul; he values himself unreservedly as a unique manifestation of the divine and needs no possessions or status to support his ego. Whether he appears wealthy or poor he has few needs and those that he has are simple and easily satisfied. It is surely ironic that as we gain in personal power and magical ability we are less and less attracted to the pursuit of goals which we are now able to attain with relative ease. Absolute freedom is the underlying need of the magus. The freedom to be who he wishes to be twenty four hours a day.

He no longer works in order to earn a living. His work is what he chooses to do in pursuit of his spiritual path. His responsibility is to be himself; no more or less. He is not concerned how others react to him. He may appear to be rude, eccentric, normal, kindly, charming perhaps even dull and boring but he will always be himself. Unless, of course, he chooses not to be.

Personal Mastery and the Training of the Magus Within

CHAPTER
13

SPIRITUAL LAWS

1. THE LAW OF CREATION

It is a universal law of the Cosmos that matter is created by and organises itself in accordance with the instructions communicated to it by thought. Its corollary, the Law of Chaos, states that, in the absence of thought, matter becomes disorganised, formless and dissipates into the void. From a slightly different perspective, the Law of Creation is also the Law of Love, the principle which binds together the disparate parts of the whole. Thus every part of the cosmos is a manifestation of thought, an extension of the Universal Consciousness or God.

2. THE LAW OF SUPPLY

We live in a universe capable of supplying all our needs. There is an inexhaustible supply. This is readily observable even on the physical plane. The natural state is one of abundance; it is only in the accessing and distribution of that abundance do we find imperfection. The Law of Supply is a function of the Law of Creation and states that there is always an infinite supply available. To employ this Law we need as magicians to firmly embed its truth in our spiritual consciousness. We must understand and operate on the basis, not on the basis of the physically expressed limitations that our physical senses have been taught to perceive, otherwise the objects we bring into manifestation will conform to those limitations

3. THE LAW OF POWER

The Law of Power states that power is the product of consciousness. We are powerful to the extent that we comprehend and act on the premise that our power is a function of our alignment with spiritual law and with the underlying divine spark within. Power consciousness involves the recognition that where we are right now is the product of our own (perhaps poorly regulated and adjusted) power and that we do have the power to change our circumstances. Power consciousness is the acceptance of responsibility; the turning away of needless help which serves to disempower by its assertion that we are in need.

4. THE LAW OF ONE

There is an underlying unity in all things; a single mind or consciousness, which we may call God. Our individual consciousness is merely one expression of that consciousness. This universal mind manifests through the intermediary of individual consciousnesses. Likewise, the individual consciousness manifests through the intermediary of the universal mind. Since the cosmic One manifests its consciousness in and through matter absolutely all thought impacts on the physical plane.

5. THE LAW OF BENEVOLENCE

Recognition that we are One means that we fight against the very structure of the cosmos when we try to create or sustain hostility. In doing so, we can but harm ourselves as part of the One. Certainly, we can do harm through thought. Negative thoughts can impact equally as efficiently as positive thoughts. But when we deliberately set out with the intention to cause harm - when our conscious will is employed rather than our inexperience and lack of discipline - we work directly against very powerful forces represented by the Law of One; we fight an uphill battle and sooner or later those forces overwhelm us.

When, however we live and work in the consciousness of our divine heritage and in accordance with spiritual law then the universe opens up to assist us. We suddenly join forces with the very weight of the cosmos to create extraordinary results. The universe is a benevolent force; it has to be, for it is our playground. What we have to learn to do is to operate it correctly.

6. THE LAW OF KARMA

"As ye sow, so ye shall reap". This Law is not a Law or an operation designed or functioning to punish us for our sins. It is merely the neutral, the non judgemental spiritual process which serves to correct imbalances within the material plane. Karma 'rewards' effort exerted in accordance with spiritual law by manifesting in this and subsequent lifetimes opportunities, abilities and events which represent the flowering of that effort. Thus great effort in several lives to master the intricacies of music might produce a child musical prodigy in a subsequent life. Likewise, Karma 'punishes' effort not exerted in accordance with spiritual law by manifesting blocks, disabilities, problems and events which represent repeated opportunities to correct our previous incorrect responses and the associated lack of clarity in our perception. Thus those that are prone to employing violence to achieve their ends in their present lifetime might in the next find themselves in a position where they suffer intimidation by the threat of violence.

Notice that the karmic corrective response is never, at least to start with, quite as painful as the original error act. But, if the karmic opportunities to correct our poor perception and resulting misdeeds are not grasped when they are offered, then the problems or situations offered us to work on simply get larger and larger until ultimately we get utterly devastated by their weightiness and a full scale crisis ensues

As we gradually, almost certainly over many lifetimes, learn to iron out the major swings in our responses to the karmic lessons imposed upon the major swings in our responses to the karmic lessons imposed upon us there comes a time when most if not all karmic correction can be undertaken in the same lifetime. And during such a lifetime, as this process continues, we find that the those who have very little karmic debt begin to repay it almost as soon as it arises, sometimes within an hour or two of the offending incident. Those experiencing this level of immediacy may be coming to the end of their obligatory incarnations. However, they may merely have been able to discharge their karmic debt only in one specific area, in which case immediacy will only apply to any new debts incurred in that specific area.

7. THE LAW OF TIMING

When we find that obstacles continually present themselves to us this is usually an indication that our sense of timing is out. It normally suggests that there are certain personal changes that have to take place before we can readily accomplish what we intend to achieve.

It is almost always the spiritual novice, eager for immediate results, that underestimates the length of the road ahead. That impatience leads them to ignore the amount of energy they will need to apply, the lessons that will have to be learned and the corrections to their perception that will need to occur before the progress that they look for can be made. For the work discussed in this book is all, in a sense, preparatory work. It is work which removes obstructions. It is work which clears the way and until that work has been completed the cosmos will not swing round to assist our practical aspirations.

When we screw up, when we fail to achieve what we have set our heart on it is generally because we have undertaken insufficient preparatory work. As soon as sufficient preparatory work has been undertaken the cosmos suddenly opens up to us. Whereas before there would be obstacles and obstructions, suddenly the Way is clear and free. We are able to make dramatic strides forward with seemingly little effort.

That we are together One demands a certain generosity of spirit of us as individuals. Our place in that Oneness cannot be reconciled with miserliness. Any deliberate impediment or blockage in the outward flow of energy from us cuts us off from the great spiritual river in which we live and move and have our being. If we fail to use productively an item that has a use, we impede that flow. If we are ungenerous with those that we meet on our Way, we impede that flow. If we knowingly exploit others, or the earth and thereby fail to at least restore the energy we have taken then we impede that flow. And as we cut ourselves off from the flow so the flow to us diminishes also; we create a vicious circle of diminishing output and input until we find ourselves in a very materialistic and unsatisfying backwater.

It is incumbent on each of us as expressions of the One to swim out to the middle of the great river of energy and let it flood to and through us and on to others. It is rather like basic economics. Let us take a £10.00 note passing from hand to hand in a group of 10 people. If the note passes through every person once in the space of a year, the income of every person in that year will merely be £10.00. If, however, the speed of movement of the £10.00 note is increased so that it passes around the group 10 times in the course of the year, the income of everyone in the group rises to £100.00. But all it takes is one person in the group to hang on tightly to the note for the year and the income of all others is reduced to nil. The message here is not to be spiritually or materially miserly. Keep the energy moving through you. One simple illustration of this Law in action is to leave a place better than you find it. Often this can be achieved by a gesture as simple as placing a sweet paper in a rubbish bin.

Personal Mastery and the Training of the Magus Within

CHAPTER
14

CONCLUSION

I believe that very few books inspire more than just a few of their readers into taking effective action to change the course of their lives. If this book can inspire just a few of those who, like me, have strayed and lost their way in the world, then I am well pleased.

But this will not be an easy option for them. Most people dearly want an instant answer to their problems, a quick fix that will divert their attention away from the stark reality that only they have the power to help themselves. For if you do wish to welcome in your transcendent qualities then I have to tell you that there is no alternative but for you to actually do the work. No amount of psychic readings or messages from the spirit world will help you unless you are prepared one day to seize the power in your life and take action to live it as a conscious and willing creator. I am minded to repeat Gurdjieff's words when he says that ordinary efforts do not count; only super efforts count. For ordinary efforts equate merely to the day to day efforts that we make as we go about our daily lives, and where have they got us? Literally anything is possible for you, but the work must be done; the effort made, the fear confronted, the commitment made and the truth spoken if you wish to welcome on your team the magus within.

PERSONAL MASTERY
COURSES & WORKSHOPS

Please write to the publisher for details of John's
current program of workshops and courses

If you have a group of 20 people or more John will
travel to your district and present a dynamic and
exciting day or weekend workshop

John is also available to give lectures and demonstrations